HAITI, WYCLEF JEAN & THE SCAVENGERS

Jacques Guillaume
&
Jean Jocelyn

iUniverse, Inc.
Bloomington

Haiti, Wyclef Jean & The Scavengers

iUniverse books may be ordered through booksellers or by contacting:

iUniverse
1663 Liberty Drive
Bloomington, IN 47403
www.iuniverse.com
1-800-Authors (1-800-288-4677)

ISBN: 978-14502-8687-9 (pbk)
ISBN: 978-1-4502-8688-6 (ebk)

Printed in the United States of America

iUniverse rev. date: 1/25/2011

Haiti Cherie…

Introduction

It is with a heavy heart that I tell you today that the board of elections in Haiti has disqualified me from my run for the presidency of the country. Though I disagree with the ruling, I respectfully accept the committee's final decision, and I urge my supporters to do the same. We must all honor the memories of those we've lost—whether in the earthquake, or at anytime—by responding peacefully and responsibly to this disappointment.

I was inspired to run for president because I know Haiti can become great with the right leadership, and I believe I could be that leader; but, ultimately, we must respect the rule of law in order for our island to become the great nation we all aspire for it to be.

I want to assure my countrymen that I will continue to work for Haiti's renewal; though the board has determined that I am not a resident of Haiti, home is where the heart is—and my heart has and will always be in Haiti. This ruling just tells me that I can't officially seek the office of president. More importantly, there is no one who can tell me to stop my work in Haiti, and there is no one who could. I think of my daughter, Angelina, and it makes me want to redouble my efforts to help give all the children in Haiti better days.

I also want to honor the memory of my father, a minister; I know that he would tell me that even though I've faced a setback, I must continue in all my good-faith efforts to help Haiti turn a corner to a better and brighter future. Do not think that my role in the future of Haiti is over; it's just a different role than I had anticipated it to be.

Rest assured, this isn't the end of my efforts to help improve my beloved country but only marks a new beginning.

Wyclef Jean[1]

Contents

SECTION I:
WHO WILL LEAD?

CHAPTER 1
Lesson from History

IN A WAY I WISH we could see that we are no longer in a position to wish for the possibilities of goodness. We are at a crossroad. Haiti no longer has options for choosing to love and care for its people and the country. Haitians can no longer hope that our leaders will find the common decency to govern for the well-being of the country.

I remember a time when I left this beautiful island, when it was not the best, but there was a sense of caring kindness amidst the terrible history of the island. Haitians are the most gentle and loving people. There was a time when we lived side by side. The streets were clean and the people loved their land. What is amazing is that the same Haitians are still there. The people who have survived this terrible quake are the most humble people that you will ever meet.

Haitians love, in some sense, beyond comprehension. If there were a group who could walk with angels, then Haitians would be it. Haitians are affectionate and docile people, living with a constant hope for a better tomorrow. We only know peace, we only know love, and yet, in a way, our humanity has been abused by the worst of our nature residing forever more in our leaders. So I write and I cry; my people will always suffer. In my life, we may never see Wyclef Jean as our president, or the likes of him.

You see, I have learned this is an ugly world. The people with good hearts and the ones with unconditional love, at the same time suffer miserably. Where is our Nelson Mandela, Mahatma Gandhi, Rev. Martin Luther King, Jr. President Bill Clinton or where is our President Barack Obama? Why must our people suffer? What if we could dream and Wyclef Jean could be president, and he could sing songs, and Haitians could once again laugh and dance? What if we could be in the news daily and our beautiful island could be released from the seemingly curse of permanent suffering.

Our history has been written in the blood and sweat of the gentle people, the hardworking farmers seeking a life, and the gentle merchants in the streets balancing a sack of goods on their heads and walking miles and miles looking for life. The people suffer and God looks down upon us and one day a hurricane or an earthquake will wipe out nearly half of the population in our constant state of misery. What have we done in this terrible history, where an inkling of goodness still often exists? Have our people stuck our thumb at God or is it the state of the little people with a good heart to continue suffering while living in what could be a paradise of deep riches and beauty?

Please explain why we cannot have a leader who loves the country and every Haitian as one. Why can't we have a sense of brotherhood and love each other? What is in our history that shows that we have committed a mortal sin? Please tell me why the streets must remain so dirty and why the well-to-do Haitian walks by without noticing the poor merchant who is trying to survive. Why can't anyone assemble us into a group to clean the streets, create good schools and care for our people? Please erase the terrible history from my mind, and tell me that the possibility for goodness still exists.

One of the greatest tragedies in our country is the lack of trust stored deep within our psyche. We are such beautiful people, yet we see each other through a stained glass covered with abuse and mistreatment. Being raised under the Duvalier regime for at least three decades has taught us in so many ways not to trust one another. During the dictatorship of Duvalier, we were raised to keep our mouth shut and never to express ourselves overtly to strangers, or even to people we knew. The stigma was that you never knew who was going to turn you in. We were raised with fear as a systematic way for the government to stay in power forever.

In those days, the saying was that Duvalier was elected president "for life." With on-going fear, "social gathering" became almost impossible, not to mention any revolt against the government. Our generation was raised in complete fear. We were raised to always be careful about what we said. We could never say anything negative about the government because you never knew who was working undercover. We did not trust one another. Our parents kept reminding us to keep our views to ourselves or we might disappear forever.

During the last few years of the Duvalier dictatorship regime, I was still in high school. You could not even joke about the government, or a paramilitary group like the "Tonton Macoute," because there was a fear that a classmate could report you to his parents or to someone who was working for the government. Even when we were on the phone, our communication was very brief because we never knew who was tapping the line.

Moreover, there was music that we could not play or even sing along with on the street like that of "Manno Charlemagne, Les Frere Parents, etc." If any of these bands were playing a concert, you went at your own risk because armed bandits would terrorize everyone who attended the concert. Some of the bands were in exile for a very long time. If you disagreed or spoke up against the Duvalier regime, the government could throw you in jail, torture or kill you, or send you into exile. Once you were incarcerated, your family would never be able to find you.

When I was in high school, I remember there was a play that was very popular, but also very undercover. It was the story of a single mother who raised her only son Jackie. Jackie was a very brilliant boy and he studied very hard. He would often study with his friends at a public place for group study. They were studying trigonometry. While they were studying and discussing sinus and cosinus functions, a "Tonton Macoute" was passing by. He overheard the boys talking about the evil within the government structure and communism as an option. The "Tonton Macoute," who may not have had an elementary education, had no clue what the boys were studying. He could only hear their comments about the government at times being corrupt and the talk of communism. Jackie was thrown in jail for studying communism. He was tortured and was never heard from again.

At that time, Duvalier was extremely against communism for many reasons. Duvalier had to go after the communist ideology head-on because that was the only way he was able to borrow funds from the World Bank, the International Monetary Fund (IMF), and the Inter-American Development Bank (IDB). He had to prove that he was against communism 100 percent.

Despite all of this turmoil, we still had friends. We respected the curfew and kept to our own business. We could only discuss school and personal stuff. We did get together sometimes for group study. We had some people that we could trust, like some of our instructors when we knew where they stood politically. We used to make fun of some of the people in the government without mentioning names or we would joke in parables.

Some of my classmates used to form small study groups of five to 10 students and go to each other's houses. We were quite close with the sole purpose of passing the state exams and continuing on for a higher education. We became very close and formed a united front who stood together, fought together, and were loyal in the struggle for our rights.

Now it is time that we have a leader who sees and understands the needs of the Haitian people. We need a leader who believes in helping the country, a leader who is not there to pad his own pockets, who is there to fight for the powerless and all Haitians. Haitian people deserve basic humanitarian treatment, including security, jobs, shelter, farming projects, functioning hospitals, and everything else that is vital to life. The Haitian people do not ask for a lot. They are begging for the government to implement programs that will help the majority to live better. A good government is very critical for the country to advance.

Haitian people are hardworking and tough. They always believe in a better tomorrow. Haitian people have been betrayed too many times, especially by the priest who promised so much and delivered so little. Former exiled President Jean-Bertrand Aristide was a priest and came from the masses. He betrayed the Haitian people in immeasurable ways. He had the power and the popularity to do wonders for Haiti, but instead he was lead into corruption and misdeeds.

Haitians have witnessed too much abuse and too many misdeeds by crooked politicians. It is hard for Haitians to trust any politicians now. We all know that no single person can save Haiti. It is everyone's responsibility to save the country, but we need a strong leader who can inspire the Haitian people to take the future of their country into their own hands. We need a leader who can turn things around. We do not expect changes to occur overnight, but we do expect the country to be on the right path from day one. There is no room for trial and error. There is no room for hatred among leaders and the people. When we let our differences dictate our path, we all lose. Au contraire, let's use our differences to better ourselves. We are one people and one nation under God. We can and must put our heads together to save a sinking ship before it is too late.

Chapter 2
Haitians Must Save Haiti

WHAT IS THE MEANING OF caring? What does it mean to truly care and hope to make a difference in the lives of the average Haitian? There are many organizations working in Haiti and contributing in many important ways. The efforts of the many volunteers must be applauded in reference to the tragedy, which exploded in our country in January 12, 2010. No matter how one helps in Haiti, the sense of dignity and pride of the Haitian people must never be overlooked. Anyone helping in Haiti will tell you that no one will ever see a people so full of pride amidst the suffering of the worst kind.

Do the various organizations which try to help in Haiti understand and respect the sense of pride and dignity of the Haitian people? Are they mindful of the need to restore hope and paint a picture of a better tomorrow for the Haitian people? According to an article published by Jo Piazza in the Cable News Network (CNN), a model of this understanding comes across in the organization created by Wyclef Jean in Yéle.

"In 2005, Haitian-born and Brooklyn-raised musician Wyclef Jean created the grassroots charity organization Yéle Haiti. The former member of the Grammy-winning group The Fugees coined the term Yéle in a song and imbued it with the meaning, 'a cry for freedom.'"

"The purpose of the organization has been, from its inception, to restore pride and hope to the Haitian people through projects that will allow citizens to ultimately help themselves, such as the creation of scholarships, support for the arts, food distribution and emergency relief."[2]

It is important to understand that the attention paid in restoring pride in the Haitians is crucial. Yéle, and the understanding that this organization and its mission bring forward, must be part of the efforts in Haiti. The focus must be on understanding that through the pain and suffering of the Haitian people there is always a sense of survival and strength for their ability to help themselves in the future. The future of Haiti must always be part of humanitarian contributions with the goal of providing assistance to the people of Haiti to eventually strive on their own.

Haitians are a people with great internal wealth and resilience established by their sense of pride in themselves, in each other and in their country's history. No matter what the circumstances, we walk with our heads held high. Our beautiful history and the struggle for dignity and greatness are always part of our being. We are a great people, a nation of survivors, always struggling against great odds. Our ability to always find hope and our pride in ourselves is our greatest sense of strength.

In no way does the organization created by Wyclef Jean claim to be better or claim to do a more miraculous job than any other non-profit organization working in Haiti. The important thing is the need to assure that the help is intertwined with a sense of respect for the future and strength of the Haitian people. This crucial understanding of the pride of the average Haitian may seem to be of little importance, but in reality any efforts to help must be based on inspiring the Haitian people to take care of themselves. It is always necessary to understand that within the pain and suffering exist a people who have a great deal to contribute to society as a whole. Their sense of history and pride in themselves must never be forgotten. Wyclef Jean elevates this pride in his description of the average Haitian in his music and words. He highlights this sense of well-being in the article published in the January issue of Cable News Network (CNN) Entertainment titled, *Wyclef Jean helping through 'Yéle Haiti' by* Jo Piazza.

> "I see old women with large bags of rice on their heads and men on street corners selling sugarcane and mangos, all just trying to survive with a strong sense of pride," Jean said in a statement on the group's Web site. "Walking past a church in my village, I hear the congregation singing an appeal to God to hear their cries and grant deliverance to Haiti. Through experiences like this, I sense where my mother and my father got their strength. Now the whole country needs to reach deep into the spirit and strength that is part of our heritage". [3]

Wyclef Jean reminds us of the importance of always realizing that Haitians are a great people. Through our suffering and enormous uncertainty, the Haitian people have always maintained a sense of dignity and greatness. Only by looking through the lenses of the average Haitian engaged in normal life, and watching very closely the melancholy, can one decipher the strength and resilience of the Haitian heart. Capturing this sense of pride allows the Yéle organization to contribute while knowing the future of the people lies within their own strength and well-being.

Many have contributed and done a great job in Haiti. Their efforts and contributions must be applauded. But it is important for those who are working in Haiti to be sure that their contributions are also done according to the standards set by Wyclef Jean for the Yéle foundation. As Jean said, "The objective of Yéle Haiti is to restore pride and a reason to hope, and for the whole country to regain the deep spirit and force that is part of our heritage."[4]

This important focus cannot be forgotten. While helping Haiti, there must always be a sense that this is a great people and their future must always be kept in sight and formed on a day when the Haitian people can help themselves. The Haitian spirit of never giving up, always looking toward the future and expecting better days must be part of the struggle for all who would help our people.

The misconception could exist that Haiti is a poor island and that all Haitians suffer great psychological trauma and have lost their sense of well-being. This mindset is highly mistaken. Though the pain and suffering may often be deep, there is always a pride, a sense of well-being, and a sense of personal dignity.

A better understanding of this idea lies in Wyclef Jean, himself. In him you see the joy, the laughter, the grandeur, and the sense of greatness that is the sentiment of the average Haitian. It is in our heart to feel that we are great and that we should share our pride and joy with others. Haitians are not poor in a larger sense. Haitians are the grandest people on the planet. They are a people who are larger than life, who live with poverty in the most dignified manner. They dress like movie stars walking home while poverty creeps all around them. They debate the issues of the day like scholars, always with an opinion of how to improve or make a difference in their lives. If only you really knew these people called Haitians! Our sense of pride is beyond measurement. If only God would bless this people with a chance at a decent life again!

As poverty rips though the very foundation of this nation, and leader after leader has drained everything away, the Haitian people remain filled with dignity and pride in their culture and heritage.

Wyclef Jean as president is a dream. Haitians have always lived a life of hope, always thinking that tomorrow will be a better day. This man who has it all is always coming back loving the people of this island. He has done a beautiful job being the ambassador for our island and he will always represent Haiti to its very core. The same richness and sense of pride embodies the average Haitian, who is always hopeful and looking toward a better day.

No one does a better job representing us to the world than our own Wyclef Jean. His smile is full blown, and there is no holding back or saying I am afraid. No longer is there care about what the world thinks, but only care about living and loving as Haitians, and always with a caring heart. Wyclef Jean tells us to be Haitian, Haitian to the very core of our being. Do not hold anything back. Do not pretend to be something that you're not. Let the Creole flow. Let them see, let them know that you are forever Haitian.

Please understand that we have our own Wyclef Jean hiding deep inside. Haitians are beautiful people with laughter and joy to share with the world. But, the pain and suffering which still exist in our homeland has remained a very troubling fact.

We cannot tell a half truth. Our people need long term financial assistance. Our country has been devastated and our people suffer so much. But our love of life and living cannot be subdued. We will live, no matter how much the next politician takes from us. The people of Haiti will always be gentle and loving. And if you are ever fortunate to meet a Haitian, you will feel forever blessed with the love you receive.

So we are rich, but we may also be always poor. Why it is that people with such beautiful hearts cannot find justice in their politicians? In the age of Obama, when anything is possible, there remains a small hope that somehow something grand will happen and the politicians will finally start resembling the beauty of the people of Haiti.

CHAPTER 3
Wyclef Jean Is One of Us

HAVE YOU READ THE VARIOUS articles and the many opinions on the best solutions for Haiti? An important realization is that there have always been many points of view about what the best options for Haiti are. Many pundits have made their predictions and stated their opinions about what path would lead to the perfect outcome for our beloved little island of Hispaniola. Ironically, most of the people with all of these various ideas of what Haitians should do have never even been to Haiti. Among the sea of pundits, the rare minority have actually been to the island for less than a couple of days at best to research articles they could have easily plagiarized from Wikipedia.

In fact the best thing that could happen in Haiti is if Haitian politicians could care and learn to somehow appreciate their fellow countrymen or if they could somehow realize that the money given by foreign donors to help the people is not for their pockets to pass around and gain favors and political clout among the ruling classes.

Obviously, if the politicians can learn not to use Haiti as their own private little bank account, this would do wonders for our little country. If they can somehow realize that Haitians are their people who they must serve, rather than they themselves, things would start to improve. Think about the impact this would have on the future of the country. Naturally, the country would be in much better condition if many of the so called leaders of Haiti would accept their responsibilities and do what is right for the benefit of Haiti. Haiti would certainly not be the poorest country in the western hemisphere.

However, these various wishes and great ideas have very little chance of success when the rules are written to exclude all people from the outside. This is a condition that is created to keep the same group of people in charge. The objective of the electoral process in place currently is not to ensure that the most qualified person to benefit Haiti wins. What the system is designed to do is to maintain control by a selected few on the island and to prevent anyone from outside the group gaining control. No one seems to care for the well-being of the 99 percent of Haitians who continue to suffer through abject poverty. This is not news to those in the know. Indeed, members of the American government have pointed out flaws in the Haitian political process: Congresswoman Maxine Waters' letter released December 23, 2009 to René Préval - President of Haiti, stated "concerns about the decision of Haiti's Provisional Electoral Council (CEP) to exclude more than a dozen political parties from the Parliamentary elections scheduled for February and March 2010. I am concerned that these exclusions would violate the right of Haitian citizens to vote in free and fair elections and that it would be a significant setback to Haiti's democratic development."[5]

The problem is that even with challenges like these being issued, those in power have no problem allowing the people to continue to suffer and simply do not care if billions of dollars are not released from the government to help the people. Their attitude is that the people can suffer and they will maintain the status quo as long as necessary to ensure their continued political survival and economic luxury. The idea is to ensure that the same one percent governs the country. The importance of controlling the country by a small group of elite outweighs the important need of the people.

The rules are written to exclude all Haitians who have left the country, people with any kind of political disagreement, and those who may have espoused a different idea of caring for the people and making a difference in their lives. They pay no attention to the country right next door, which seems to flourish completely beyond Haiti, namely the Dominican Republic. This is a country where the leaders have realized that those who have left the country to make a living and have educated themselves and have learned from developed nations can benefit their home country tremendously.

The Haitian electoral process was written to ensure that only those in Haiti who have been part of the process, and who have stayed there and used the system to take from the people, are on top of the charts and will have the only chance to compete. This assures that once again the people of Haiti are left out of the process and the political elite can continue with their monopoly of power.

From this very process, Wyclef Jean was nominated to be a representative of Haiti to the world, to be an ambassador who would remind other nations of the suffering and dire need of Haitians. The decision was somehow reached that this man had stayed away from Haiti too long and had not fulfilled the requirements to have lived in Haiti for five consecutive years. This concept is so full of ambiguity that the council can always find ways to invalidate the candidacy of anyone who has stepped outside of Haiti for even a day. This is just another way that the political elite can keep the cards stacked in their favor.

No one asked the question as to why Wyclef Jean was truly barred from running. Jean has never given up his Haitian citizenship and always remained within the boundary of

Haitian laws by maintaining his citizenship. He always has been a citizen of Haiti. This was the man who was part of the system because he wanted to give something back to his people. He has always maintained one foot in the United States, and one foot inside Haiti, looking to make a difference. President René Préval for very good reason name Wyclef Jean, Haiti's ambassador to the world. In reality, Wyclef Jean symbolized Haiti and the struggle to survive and exist within a very difficult and often troubling crisis.

Wyclef Jean, from the start, has a history of giving and being there for the people of Haiti. He is a man who has done plenty and yet never once flaunted his political ambitions. He gave to the people because these were his countrymen, members of his culture who were in need of help. Jean saw the importance of giving back, and of loving and caring. His constant trips back to his homeland, every part of his conscience and his psyche, as if his need for survival depended on doing well for his people in a country where 99 percent of the people are living in abject poverty and the government seems to offer very little care to improve the lives of the people.

Wyclef Jean, son of a preacher, lives and understands the concept of giving and having a mission to make a difference in the lives of people. In a sense, Jean may have followed in his father's footsteps, being a steward of the gospel, preaching the good news of loving, and caring and making a difference in the lives of people. Jean has lived with the concept of hitting the pavement and preaching the good news in his own way with a guitar on hand, Jean has been a preacher in his own right, delivering good news and reminding the people of Haiti that there is hope after the fall.

Haiti will survive and indeed has a possibility for greatness if Haitians can only have hope for one more day and believe that their island has been given another chance. Jean's life was not established by a need just to live and survive. His life has been guided by a higher mission of giving back and a constant striving to find ways to improve the lives of the people of Haiti. One example of this was his creation of the Yéle organization.

In no time at all, after Wyclef Jean announced his candidacy for the presidency, the many pundits began to explain the various reasons to oppose him. Yes, naturally, Jean is a great musician, a great humanitarian, and a great human being, but in their words he may not have the capacity to serve the country as its next leader. Why not let him run? The easiest answer is that he would probably have won.

The Haitian people love Wyclef Jean. Everyone loves a favorite famous son, but beyond this, he was a humanitarian, a man who spent his life doing his best to make a difference. But somehow, he was the one singled out and considered unqualified. Indeed, in disqualifying Wyclef Jean, Haiti's Provisional Electoral Council (CEP) knocked out of the race the front runner, the one the people would have likely chosen.

No one asked questions of any of the other leaders. No articles were written extensively about any of the other candidates and the reasons for their qualification. This did not matter, just as the right of the 99 percent of Haitians did not matter. Their suffering and pain is no longer on top of the list.

The question was never pondered about the current leaders, who have ruled over a country where the people seem to be forever frozen in a state of constant poverty, and when it does not matter how much money is given to Haiti. The money flows with the wind and the people stay mired in poverty and despair. As an article in the British Broadcast Corporation (BBC), *Haiti Country Profile*, stated, "Meanwhile, Haiti's most serious underlying social problem, the huge wealth gap between the impoverished Creole-speaking black majority and the French-speaking minority, 1% of whom own nearly half the country's wealth, remains unaddressed."[6] It is almost as if somehow those on the very top decided that these people with their dark skin, speaking Creole, are not worth being cared about and their well-being is unimportant. The concept of starving and living with very little seems to have no sway on those in control of the country.

The focus of this election does not seem to have been centered on the needs of the people. Who can assure that Haiti remains on center stage, that the eyes of the world remain on Haiti, and that 99 percent of Haitian the population does not fall through the crack again and the people continue to suffer?

Where were the articles evaluating the other candidates and scrutinizing their qualifications and seeing what if anything they would do for the Haitian people? Could it be that many of the other candidates are related to some politician or group, which has stolen from Haiti? Could it be that many of the candidates on the ballot have somehow been part of the paralysis that has existed where a country seems to have no desire to promote industry or anything for the masses, and where 99 percent of the people suffering from abject poverty and no one seems to care.

The important question must be asked: Why do we only learn of the many reasons, why this individual, who the people love, and who has done so much for them already, is the one who would not be the perfect president? Or why he would not be the Obama for Haiti? The pundits give their various justifications. No one talks of the electoral process which assures that the ruling class in Haiti stays in power, absorbing every dime that is given to the country and passing it around among themselves. The perfect solution is someone from the outside who would reshuffle the process so that the individuals speaking Creole who are from the people would be directly responsible to the people.

What was the criterion that was used to judge Wyclef Jean lacking? Was there a need to compare Wyclef to the other candidates? Did it matter that his qualifications were far superior to the many of the other candidates who followed the same lines as various other Haitian leaders of the past, taking from the people and given anything back? No, this fact was not important. What was important was to level many reasons why Wyclef Jean would not make a perfect president in Haiti?

No one cared to mention the fact that Wyclef Jean was one of our own, the one who the people had been waiting for. The one who had done more than all of the other candidates combined for the sake of the Haitian people. No mentioned was made of his wonderful humanitarian work and the fact that this man had put Haiti on the map long before the magnitude 7.0 earthquake on January 12, 2010.

Here was an individual the people would want to lead them. Here was their front runner, their Obama, their dream come true, the one who was one of them. He was the one who could speak their language, a man who would not speak French to the Haitian people on radio and television, a language that 90 percent of the people do not understand. He was truly from the people, a Creole speaking son of a preacher, a man the people of Haiti could understand and trust. The people would have nothing to worry about because they knew that Wyclef Jean would be speaking their language, would know them and would make a difference in their lives.

Why is Wyclef Jean not our beloved? Why do we hear criticism after criticism? I do not understand the concept that does not give the man a chance to lead his people and make a difference. I remember when Barack Obama was running for the presidency of the United States. Many said that this country would not elect an African American president, not in my heart, I knew from the minute that he ran that his chances were as good as anyone's in the race.

You see, this is the beauty of American-style democracy; the idea of being given a chance, a chance to make a difference, a chance to elect a man who thought can take us down a course that is righteous. In no way do we suggest that the outcome of a Wyclef Jean presidency would be a golden era of prosperity without challenges, nor do we compare to our President Barack Obama to Wyclef Jean. Our points are, why not provide the possibility? Why not give the people a chance to pick who they believe will be the best to run the country?

The facts are, no matter what anyone says, Wyclef Jean will always be a Haitian in its truest form. Wyclef Jean did not promote his Haitians roots when it was popular to do so. Instead, from the very start, he embraced the common Haitians, the ones that the elites ruling class cannot understand or communicate with, the ones who some believe do not matter. That has always been my problem with those in the so-called upper class. You must understand that those who speak Creole, those who make their living through struggle and living by the crumbs that fall from the table of the elite, they are and forever will be Haitian.

I must embrace and compliment my Haitian brother, Wyclef Jean, for being true to the majority of us, for being true to the ones that we must help. We cannot always think only of ourselves and what we can gain from every situation. There are times when we must look at the little ones and ask, "What can I do for my fellow Haitians?"

This election cannot be about the upper class; this election cannot be about taking all of the generosity that has come from around the world to help our people rebuild for the benefit of the elite. This election has to be about the little ones. It has to be about those who speak Creole, to whom the educated French of the elite is a foreign language.

Wyclef Jean says, we must speak English and that French has gotten us nowhere. Is he speaking the truth, is he telling it like it is? Let's be honest and ask ourselves, what are we afraid of? Are we afraid that this could actually challenge the youth and help them develop in an area that can benefit them? Do you see the many jobs that leave the U.S. and flow to India and many other developing countries? The answer is that the people in these other countries have been given the opportunity to learn skills that are useful and moreover, they always speak English and are able to do business with the English speaking world.

We must truly ask ourselves if it would benefit the Haitian youth to learn English. Does the question that Wyclef Jean asked speak to the benefit of the Haitian people? Does that not matter? Does it not matter that our membership in the Francophone world has gotten us nowhere? Or, is it all right to speak in flowery words, while the people starve and no one cares about their well-being.

Wyclef Jean will forever be one of us, and I truly believe that we need a president who looks out for the interests of the rich, poor, middle class, but all Haitians. I do not say that the country cannot function without Wyclef Jean, but I do say that whoever wins the presidency has to be a man who embraces the values of Wyclef and his vision of a new Haiti, where the status quo is no longer acceptable. As President Obama said, "Doing the Same Thing Over and Over, and Expecting Different Results!"[7] These words of our own President Obama ring so true.

Haiti has to change. The same ideas will not work and, most important of all, a leader has no business speaking French to the common people. A true leader for our island will look the people in the eyes and tell them in their own language what he plans to do for them and not deliver the same old lines. I've heard over and over and nothing is more insulting to our people than to listen to a Haitian speaking French, when they know that this is a foreign tongue. Creole is the language of Haiti. Be straight with the people and tell them the truth in their own language. Creole is spoken and Creole is understood.

SECTION II:
SCAVENGERS

CHAPTER 4

Restoring Trust and Integrity

ONE OF THE MAJOR PROBLEMS in today's Haiti is the lack of trust and integrity in our government officials and leaders. The Haitian people have been oppressed for decades by Haitian leaders who constantly take advantage of the least fortunate ones. Many of our leaders are waiting for their turn to rob, fill their pockets, and flee the country.

Lack of integrity makes all Haitians suffer both inside and outside of Haiti. It is a must that we reestablish Haitian integrity in Haiti and across the globe. To do this effectively we as Haitians need to help one another. We need to come together as one people inside and outside of Haiti to lift our country up. We need to rebuild the country and it takes all of us. Of course, we need a leader who can talk the talk and walk the walk. We need a leader who can model the way and inspire others to follow. We need a leader who can communicate with the Haitian people efficiently and effectively and understand their needs.

Having a well structured and trusted government is very critical in order for the country to move forward and establish a better relationship with its people and the international community. Haitians have been suffering due to lack of trust in our senior leaders. If Wyclef Jean were to be president, he would have to create a government with full transparency. His government will have to build trust from day one. He will have to show that his main concern is the Haitian people. His words, so far, have shown a path of distinction with the high possibility of achieving this objective.

In one article written in *USA Today*, titled "Wyclef Jean Offers Details on Plans for Haiti," Jean says, "The number one problem in Haiti is corruption." And, in addition to repairing the nation's infrastructure, he would make it a priority to move all of the earthquake-displaced citizens out of their makeshift tent cities and into "agrarian villages" that will provide basic necessities like food, water and shelter.[8]

Wyclef Jean's government has to earn the trust of the Haitian people and foreigners as well. He will need a team of people from different age groups and educational backgrounds. In fact, it is wonderful that he shows a willingness to do just that. Jean states, "What I learned from Nelson Mandela is [the need for] dialogue. In order to do this, you need to be coming from a neutral perspective; you need to be willing to listen to everyone's point of view."[9] The importance of having an open mind and being able to look for people with various points of view is important.

Equally important is having people who trust the rule of law. Wyclef Jean will have to adopt a zero tolerance policy toward his cabinet members. It takes only one bad apple to spoil the entire basket. He will have to find a systematic way to stop drugs and weapons from entering the country and also stop the paramilitary groups from resurfacing again. A lot of countries in the Caribbean blame Haiti for being an easy path for weapons to infiltrate into other countries or islands. The security at our ports needs to be tightened. There is an urgent need to use state of the art technology to scan containers for drugs, weapons and any other illegal products.

Individual safety has always been critical. People cannot even consider building better lives unless they feel safe. In Haiti, more than a million earthquake victims are still living in tents and other temporary shelters. The inhuman living conditions increase the risk of a precarious environment prone for injury, disease and crime. It is high time that the people living in temporary shelters be moved to permanent housing as soon as possible where their basic needs can be fulfilled. These people, mostly women and children, are the primary target for all kinds of crimes and the environment is prone to social injustice since the justice system was already handicapped and ill-prepared for this kind of environment.

Security for the Haitian people, mostly the most vulnerable ones, is a must. A lot of Haitians living abroad would love to return home to help in the rebuilding effort of their country, but they are quite concerned about their security. Haitian and non-Haitian investors may want to invest in Haiti since there is a lot of opportunity now, but security for their investment, relatives and employees is very critical. A comprehensive security plan is critical in order to attract foreign investors and donors. Can Wyclef Jean re-assure the Haitian people that security will be his top priority, compared with other candidates? Do we have any prospective leaders who are able to rally the international community to better Haiti?

> The words of Jean himself say it best. In an article in *PR Newswire* titled, "Yele Haiti's Wyclef Jean Urges Strong Call to Action as Six-Month Anniversary of Earthquake Approaches," Wyclef Jean asked the Interim Haiti Recovery Commission to release $150 million of pledged funds in the next 90 days to carry out coherent public safety and security plans addressing current violence, kidnappings,

abductions, rapes, and sexual abuse rampant in the most vulnerable communities.[10]

The goal is to turn Haiti into a law-abiding bastion. Adequate security will require constant reform in the police force. The police force is not currently adequate to provide security for the population, particularly in Port-au-Prince. The Haitian National Police Force is about 12,000 for a population over eight million people, and it is there to provide law enforcement services as well as defensive operations.

Haiti is very vulnerable at all levels, starting with security. We desperately need our army back. We all know that the previous army was highly corrupted and too politically involved. We need a more organized and better trained army. We need an army that can rescue the Haitian people during a catastrophic event such as the day of the earthquake and the days that followed. We need an army that will be there to protect civilians when they are being terrorized by gangs and thugs. We need an army that is well equipped and trained to dismantle those pockets of gangs and any other threat from within or outside. The army is needed to re-establish a sense of integrity for the Haitian people. And, we cannot reproduce the same corrupted army.

The new leader needs to have a better road map for the new army. One important aspect is to establish a clear guideline for the army versus the Haitian National Police. There used to be some confusion between the police and the army during the time of Duvalier. Of course, the duty of the police officers is law enforcement while the army's is mostly defense. We need a leader who understands this to protect the Haitian people.

There is a story of two Haitian men, Pierre and Makorel, who used to work at a factory, doing some janitorial work. They were very good friends and used to eat together. That was during the Duvalier regime. Then, Makorel decided to become a member of the "Tonton Macoute," a paramilitary group that reported directly to president Dr. Francois Duvalier, a|k|a Papa Doc. Once Makorel was hired as a Tonton Macoute, he quit his job. The two friends lost contact and of course, they did not have telephone at that time. Makorel was enrolled and trained and it is important to keep in mind that most Tonton Macoutes were very faithful to Duvalier because he was in power for life.

The Tonton Macoutes were fearless in the way they treated people. They even betrayed their own family members. It was even reported that a Tonton Macoute once turned his mother in. They terrorized the community where they lived as a way to get promoted. They were even more powerful than soldiers who were better educated. Most Tonton Macoutes were not that educated. Pierre and Makorel lost contact for a long time.

Then, one day Pierre was in the downtown area and decided to get something to eat at a restaurant. It was then that he ran into his old buddy Makorel, who was all dressed up in his Tonton Macoute uniform with his Tonton Macoute friends.

Pierre was so happy to see his old buddy Makorel and ran to shake hands with him and chat as usual. Makorel became a complete stranger. He refused to shake hands with Pierre. He pretended he never knew him. When Pierre persisted, he ended up slapping Pierre in front of everyone at the restaurant as a sign that he was not at Pierre's social rank. Makorel obviously felt that he would lower himself by shaking hands with that janitor guy who is doing a low paid job at a factory.

Makorel was now at a different social group. He felt that he was in power and Haitian people consider power, education and money as the three primary values that determine the social division in our country. To this day, I remember so vividly a favorite line of one of my 10th grade teachers, Bobby Alcendor:

"Chita pedi tanw sou ban lekol. Sonje byen neg ki chita sou menm ban bo kotew jodia, pap pale avek ou après 10 ans anko lel vin senateur, ingenieur, docteur, ministre, etc. si ou pa apran lekol."

In English this translates to, "Those students who keep wasting time at school, mark my words! The guy who sits next to you today in the same classroom will not talk to you 10 years from now once he becomes a senator, engineer, physician, minister, etc. if you do not study to better yourself."

The words make perfect sense. As teenagers, we used to joke to each other by saying, "When I become a physician, I will not talk to you any more if you do not bring yourself up."

There is a corrupt structure in the Haitian government which treats power in the most abhorrent ways. It is a structure that fails to realize that power is given to serve the people and to look out for the well-being of the majority. The political order in Haiti is such that those in power are out of control. Once they have a uniform and guns, no one can stop them. As the Kreyol saying goes, "Depi nou gen pouvwa, rwa pa kouzen nou, presiden pa bo-pen," which translates as follows, "Once we are in power, we lose respect for everyone around us." This is the mentality that must be changed for power to be shifted to the people. This is the selfish mentality that requires a strong leader like Wyclef Jean to turn the structure around.

Quality service is paramount. Change has to come from within. As Haitians, we must be willing to change the way we have been operating the government offices. Most of the jobs in Haiti are from the government offices and we need to find a better way to manage those offices, which could generate profit if they were administered efficiently and effectively.

For instance, let's say a customer submits an application

for phone service, a simple phone line. It can take more than 12 months before the government office responds. Sometimes, the office may never respond to the customer's inquiry. However, if a high profile person shows up at the telephone service office (Teleco), service may be provided within a few days if not within 24 hours. It all has to do with who you know. Why should a customer have to beg for basic phone service? It is because the infrastructure is not there to meet the entire population's needs and because the Teleco system is quite antediluvian.

If the infrastructure is not available, why not fix it? If the government is not equipped to improve the telecommunication system, the government needs to find a systematic way to improve it. It is our mindset that pushes us so far behind. My personal assessment is that the government has proven to be inefficient in the way it has been mismanaging certain government entities ranging from telecommunications to the utility services. I truly believe that the Haitian government cannot manage these entities. Things are becoming more chaotic each day.

The best and safest route is to privatize the telecommunication service (Teleco), water and electricity (EDH), garbage collection, etc. Once these entities become privatized, services will be improved significantly and customers will be treated with more respect. Of course, a lot of people will lose their jobs, mostly those who refuse to change and learn the correct way to manage these entities. The reason why the Haitian government has not been able to privatize these entities is purely political. Family members and friends might lose their jobs once the government lets go of the entities to the private sector.

Let's take a look at the utility company, EDH, for instance, and let's say the average consumer may have electricity for four to six hours a day if they are in a good location. Some people may not have any power at all. Customers receive the same kind of service for water. On average, they may have water once a day for about three hours. In some places, it may even be worse. The water is often not clean and when it rains the water becomes even dirtier.

However, there are people in Port-au-Prince who have electricity and water 24/7 given the location in which they live. The upper class, who is about one percent of the population, receives the best possible service. There are places in Port-au-Prince that do not give you the impression that you are even living in Haiti. The gap between the "haves" and the "have nots" has been expanding at a vertiginous speed in the past few decades. And, an unemployment rate of more than 80 percent has continuously aggravated the gap between the "haves" and the "have nots" over time.

In some places in Port-au-Prince, you may see more Mercedes Benz, BMWs and other exotic automobiles on the road more than you do in the United States per square miles. We all know the main reason why Haiti is so poor is not because money does not come into the country. The problem is one of distribution. A lot of money does come into the country; however, the money does not filter through the main stream. The money makes it way to offshore bank accounts outside of Haiti.

Haiti needs progressive leaders. Haiti needs Wyclef Jean or a man of his caliber who can advance the important needs of the population. We need leaders who can improve the lives of the majority. We need leaders who see the future, instead of their pockets. We need leaders who will restore integrity in the government offices. We need leaders who will hold our elected officials and government employees more accountable. We need leaders who will paint a better picture of our country. We need leader who can inspire drastic change in the way we operate and foster respect toward one another.

CHAPTER 5
What Does It Mean to be Haitian?

IF YOU ARE HAITIAN, HAVE you ever been told that you don't look Haitian? For a time, this question was something of a mystery for me. I always wondered why I was being asked such a question. What was it about my appearance that was different, that did not allow me an immediate identification with the rest of my countrymen? Was I somehow better because I was not linked with the majority of Haitians? Could I somehow maintain some independence from my people, or was I physically associated with some unknown group? Today I am dismayed when someone comments that somehow I don't look Haitian. There is no uniform physical description that fits an entire population, and we are all part of the mixture of our genetic heritage. I know and realize that I look very much Haitian, isn't like many other Haitians who are often attributed to another group because of their lack of association with the majority of Haitians. Haitians are a mixed group with many different backgrounds and have intermingled with many other races. No one can say who is Haitian and who is not based on their looks.

In a way, I, Jean-Max Jocelyn, am ashamed to say that

during my youth, deep within me, there was some sort of pride in knowing that my appearance was somehow different from that of the average Haitian. Was I somehow a superior or better person with the ability to distance myself from my brothers and sisters who were suffering? Or, was my Haitian status diluted and, somehow, not completely Haitian? Or, was I one who suffered a lower sense of self esteem since I was not able to deal with the pain and baggage associated with being a Haitian? I found myself completely unable to deal with the negative press that has always surrounded a nation full of challenges and difficulties.

What of my brothers and sisters who had no choice but to embrace their identity? What about those who had to be Haitian to receive help? What of those who, because of their pride, walked with their heads high within the pain and suffering of a broken nation for so many years? What about the poor, who were left alone to carry the baggage of being Haitian, the victims who were the last to benefit from the goodness of foreign donors? What about the so called 99 percent who continue to struggle and find life, those who have no choice but to be Haitian, through and through?

They are the true Haitians, the ones who every once in awhile cobble together in a boat to escape, and somehow deal with the difficulty of being called a refugee in a foreign land. They are all my brothers and sisters forever and just as Haitian as the Caucasian fellow that I met while serving in the U.S. Air Force, who spoke my mother's tongue of Creole and proclaimed his Haitian ancestry loud and clear.

Have you ever had to walk the halls of a school with people looking at you and calling out, "Hey, you Haitian, where is your banana boat, you refugee?" Those words forever challenged my psyche and my pride during my youth. They hurt and I felt the stinging bite of the intolerance of these words in the deepest corners of my heart. At times, I had to ask God why such a punishment was being meted out to me and to an entire people. Why must we suffer through such an ordeal? I felt like running as fast as I could and escaping the whole world. In some respects I felt utterly trapped by an identity that was so heavily associated with pain and anguish. It was then than my mind would transform my surroundings and I would escape and jump into a world where I no longer would be forced to accept this identity, this pain and the suffering of being Haitian.

My mind would wonder and I would ask myself if the old stories were true, if we had been cursed for challenging slavery, and for challenging French rule. Why had we so boldly proclaimed our freedom, and made ourselves the first free black nation in the Western Hemisphere? It was not easy in the 70's growing up Haitian and walking the streets of Miami, Florida. I often wanted to run as far, far away and I could from my Haitian identity. I tried within my own logic to find ways to masquerade and erase the very notion of being part of a Haitian group. My accent would drift from impersonating British to any exotic language I could think of, so that others could not determine my background and ancestry. I wanted to be lost and never found in the land of my birth, that beautiful island of pain and anguish. When other people would question my accent and ask where I was from, my answer would be hidden deep within my silent. I was secure in knowing that I had achieved my objective of being completely foreign, unique, and not Haitian.

In those days in my youth, I could no longer bear the suffering and the pain. My father would bear the full thrust of my arguments against identifying with my true roots and have to listen to the reasons why Haiti had done nothing for me. I would argue that Haiti had given me nothing but pain and suffering and by no means should I be forced to identify with this island of pain and turmoil. My father was my main opponent, a man who found Haiti at the center of his being and for whom being a Haitian and reveling in his identity meant almost more than life. He would challenge me with the fullness of his love and pride for his homeland, like a commander catching a deserter and announcing the crime to the squadron. In his mind, identifying with my Haitian background was a duty and, no matter what the circumstances, I must stand tall and proud and find the fullest joy in being Haitian.

But with a great deal of pain, for a long time I ran, and ran and ran. Like many Haitians who are unable to bear the pain of our suffering, I was a man without a true identity. I was lost while looking for myself and escaping the reality that among our suffering, there is greatness and strength in the backbone of our people.

Then one day, the music of a new, bold young pearl of our homeland named Wyclef Jean would change everything about me being Haitian and who I was. This was a man for whom being Haitian, like my father, was at the center of his being. For this man, accepting and admitting to his Haitian identity was not a matter of choice. Wyclef Jean would proclaim loud and clear the country of his birth and wrap himself in his identity like it was life itself. Being Haitian was like breathing air for him, and his successes and his setbacks had to be defined by it.

Wyclef Jean founded the band "The Fugees." He could have chosen another name and escaped his identity as a Haitian, instead of embracing it as one would embrace a new born child. He encircled himself with everything and anything which emphasized his Haitian origins. His proclamation gave my life a better sense of understanding who I was, and I'm sure he helped many other Haitians who were lost and suffering, trying in vain to escape from their true identity and the beauty and greatness of who we are.

Wyclef Jean reminded us that we are a nation of greatness, forever fighting for our lives and defining our existence on our own terms. When he encircled himself with the Haitian flag, his actions created a permanent line in the sand that proclaimed that he and many others like him are forever Haitian, bold and proud. Wyclef Jean, like my father, showed that it was not only acceptable to announce one's Haitian ancestry, but it was also a must, a duty of life itself to embrace and give the best of our ourselves to each other and to our homeland.

When Wyclef Jean had to decide on a name for his band, he could have picked any other name and become famous without ever embracing his Haitian identify. Instead, he settled on a term associated with the most negative connotation given to our given identify. The term "refugee" as defined by the Webster dictionary means, "To dream that you are a **refugee**, signifies your feeling of not belonging anywhere. You feel socially rejected or emotionally isolated."[11] This is a term often given to people who are lost and land where they do not belong. Jean's decision took the term "refugee," and removed the "re" and just used "Fugees" as the name of his band.

We as Haitians were familiar with all of the negative connotations associated with the term "refugee." For a time in American culture, "refugee" and "Haitians" were synonymous, as my school-aged tormenters demonstrated. Wyclef Jean, through his bravery and good heart, embraced it all and said that, yes we are refugees, but we are beautiful nevertheless. In his mind, and more through his music, Haitians became the proud, beautiful people he knew we always were, and his music helped me realize that Haitians everywhere should love every minute of our being and who we are.

The love and respect of the youth feel and nearly all Haitians for Wyclef Jean is as wide as the ocean, and this esteem is very much deserved. Jean says through his music, "Haitians, you are beautiful! Do not hide in your pain and suffering. Look at yourself, and see the beauty of the island resonating in your very being. Beauty and greatness define your very existence, underneath your pain and suffering. The island of Hispaniola gave rise to a people with their skin as dark as rubies, and some as light as snow, but nevertheless, Haitians, true and true."

Wyclef Jean embraced the reality of suffering and pain in our homeland, reminded us to look closer and see the beauty in our people and our history, and never to forget this honorable truth: that we are beautiful in more ways than one. Haitians are a people who, though living in desperate poverty, will give the very shirt off their backs to a stranger in worse need than themselves. The financially challenged Haitian who walks through the streets of Port-au-Prince, though without work and on the verge of destitution, but yet dresses like a million dollars, with a meticulously ironed shirt and wearing more French cologne than should be legally allowed. Haitians are a people whose life may have been ripped from underneath them with the most devastating of catastrophes, but they continue to find hope in the goodness of each other and the goodness of their land.

Thank you, Wyclef Jean, for reminding us to take pride in ourselves and embrace our Haitian identity with every breath we take. Thank you for reminding us to walk with our heads held high, in the fullest measure of pride, and to pass on to the next generation this identity, just as our parents did for us. This may be a simple act for some, but an enormous gesture for other who choose to look the other way. Wyclef Jean reveals a pure heart and a care for his people that know no bounds, along with a genuine love for being Haitian. It was his decision to show an affinity for the love of his people and the need to identify with our suffering in every way possible.

Wyclef Jean also showed that the most important rule in governing our little island has to start with the love of ourselves and the love of what make us unique as a people. Many of us refugees who love to travel to other lands are looking for a better chance in life, but we always identify with being a part of those beautiful people who have suffered a great deal, but yet through it all are some of the most lovable and greatest people on this earth.

The facts surrounding our lives and our history demand a show of hands and the need for all Haitians to come out of their shelters and proclaim their identity with boldness and pride. As Haitians, we can no longer just exist and move to foreign lands to support ourselves and forget the rest of our people. Like Jean's example, we must give back, no matter how we do it.

It starts with first embracing ourselves and our identity. We are a great and wonderful people. We must realize that no matter how we landed in the United States, where I now find myself, or in any other corner of the globe, we are still refugees. We will never have both feet in our host countries. We will always keep one foot in being the first free black nation in the Western Hemisphere, whose history has forever cemented our identity with the value of struggling and fighting against the odds.

Haitians have always been a fighting people who had to struggle for liberation from slavery, and for our right to self determination. We have a duty to pass on this story of the slaves who freed themselves and made a country all their own in the process.

The need for all Haitians to give back to our homeland should not be optional. We can no longer hide from our people's pain and suffering. This very day, the suffering of our people demands action; we must stand up on the side of justice, on the side of caring, and embrace everything about ourselves and our Haitian heritage. Our people and the next generation need our help to understand themselves and embrace the greatness and the possibility of achieving great deeds while being Haitian. It is time for all of us to contribute and give back to our homeland.

SECTION III:
HOPE IS ESSENTIAL

CHAPTER 6
Hope Is In Our Blood

"ESPOIRE FAIT VIVRE" IS A well-known Haitian saying, which means with hope there is life. Yes, the storm of January 12th caught the Haitian people and the world by surprise. Such human disaster was unimaginable and beyond comprehension. The world extends out to the Haitian people unconditionally. Nearly 300,000 Haitians lost their lives in a blank of an eye after the earthquake on January 12, 2010. Millions of Haitians are still living in temporary shelters. Life is extremely precarious although it was already very difficult living in Haiti before the earthquake. Life has become unbearable for the majority of Haitian families.

As Haitians, where do we go from here? How do we restore normal life for our brothers and sisters? Will the country ever go back to its normality again? Can we still be hopeful that life of the majority will improve or get back to normal? Haitians cannot stay still and expect to see changes happen in Haiti. We must pick ourselves up and dust ourselves and start rebuilding our country for better.

In order for Haiti to get back on its feet, there are a lot of things that need to be done. The next generation of leaders in

Haiti cannot afford to follow the patterns of the past in using the country for only their benefit. The steps to bring Haiti back to normality are clearly outlined by our beloved Wyclef Jean. Though the needs are many, I believe there are four basic but urgent priorities we must address first in order to begin transforming Haiti socially, politically and economically.

> • **Security**: People cannot even consider building better lives unless they feel safe. In Haiti, more than a million earthquake victims are still living in tents and other temporary encampments. The harsh and unsanitary living conditions increase the risk of injury, disease and crime. Though the ultimate goal is permanent housing, of course, we must at a minimum put people in secure shelters as soon as possible.
> • **International aid**: Foreign governments pledged $5.3 billion to Haiti after the earthquake, but only 9% of it has shown up. Haiti needs a president who can turn promises into reality—someone who will crisscross the earth and convince world leaders to deliver on their promises to the Haitian people.
> • **Job creation**: Haitians need jobs, and there are jobs to be done in Haiti. We must train a generation of engineers, tradesmen and carpenters who can improve our roads, water, sewers and other infrastructure while supporting themselves and their families. We also need to cultivate Haiti's rich culture of entrepreneurship by increasing the availability of microcredit and simplifying laws and bureaucracy.[12]
> • **Education**: Haiti is one of the poorest countries in the world, yet 90% of students must pay for school after first grade. Moving forward means changing the education system from a privilege to a birthright,

and establishing schools to teach technology and other 21st-century skills.

Haitian people are always going to school. We never stop learning. Unfortunately, most of the learning takes place outside of Haiti. We know that our Haitian brothers and sisters yearn for that back home. The opportunity is just not there. As my cousin, Lamar puts it, "Most Haitian people have so many degrees on their wall that one day they will start measuring patients' temperature."

I remember the story of a single Haitian mother who raised four boys on her own. She did not know how to read or write. She helped her kids with their homework every day. The kids never knew that their mother was illiterate. Their mother used to make them recite their lessons daily. She had a good intuition when her kids knew their lessons or not. The kids grew up to be very brilliant. Whenever the school sent documents for her to sign, she always asked her neighbor to sign it for her while the kids were in school. It was after they finished high school that they realized their mother could not even write her name. This is to show you that education is such an opportunity desired by so many in Haiti that even the uneducated one appreciates it.

Haiti needs help from all of us, mostly Haitians. It is obvious that certain skills are not available these days. Many high skilled Haitians already left Haiti to go live abroad like in Canada. Human resources are lagging behind. A process needs to set forth to train a generation of engineers, tradesmen and carpenters who can improve our roads, water, sewers and other infrastructure while supporting themselves and their families. Haiti does not have a sewage system yet. Isn't it time to build the infrastructure for a sewage system? The Haitian government and the USAID coupled with some nongovernmental organizations and the private sector can create a lot of jobs in building new roads, removing debris, or providing a safe environment for people to live. Many other nongovernmental organizations, in collaboration with the Rotary Club International, can also create a lot of street cleaning and street maintenance jobs that would hire hundreds of Haitians.

The private sector, including USAID, private banks, and the Non-Governmental Organizations (NGO) needs to provide long-term and durable assistance to small businesses. These small businesses need to have access to funds to jolt their business back on track again. Haiti needs a credible president who can turn promises into reality. Such president will have to be able to sway many world leaders and individuals from the private sector to fulfill their promises to the Haitian people after the earthquake. Haiti is in urgent need of all kinds of assistance. The need of assistance ranges from logistic to technical. In addition to all the funds that were pledged, Haiti is in desperate need for a complete debt relief from its creditors. Haiti cannot afford to even pay the interest on its debt.

It is almost hard to admit that Haiti's legacy of debt was actuated right after we became the first free black colony in the Western Hemisphere from France, and the second around the world after Ethiopia. Not only did we fight a bloody battle to gain our independence from France, but also we had to pay or agree to owe France a sum of 150 million francs (modern equivalent of $21 billion) twenty-nine years after our independence to compensate France's loss in Haiti. That was the only way France would have agreed to recognize Haiti as sovereign republic. Right from the beginning, Haiti's debt was unjust and ludicrous. Then, we had an exodus of corrupt governments who were selfish and oppressive. They never envisioned a better Haiti for its people. They only saw their inner-circle. Those Haitian leaders borrowed money left and right from the World Bank, International Monetary Fund (IMF), or Inter-American Development Bank (IDB).

Indeed, the previous debt relief initiative by IDB cancelled all Haiti's debt acquired prior to 2005. Even after the relief, Haiti acquired more debt from IDB, which may be around half of a billion dollars. Some lenders have already vowed to eliminate Haiti's debt so far this year. Haiti needs a fresh start. A fresh start that spreads at all layers in leadership, operation, administration, people' attitude, young or old, rich or poor, etc. Among everything else, all Haiti's debts need to be forgiven in order for the country to move forward. It has been said that Haiti has more NGOs per capita than any other country in the world. It is amazing to accept the fact that some estimate that nearly 2/3 of the USAID funds given to Haiti come back to a US bank through NGOs. Meanwhile, it has been noted that less than one cent of every dollar of U.S. disaster aid currently goes directly to the Haitian government, which makes perfect sense.

Moreover, we also need to cultivate Haiti's rich culture of entrepreneurship. The government, in collaboration with the private sector, needs to increase the availability of micro-credit for small entrepreneurs and simplify laws and bureaucracy. A lot of small businesses were destroyed after the earthquake. These small businesses were and will be the backbone of long-term job creation in Haiti. The working class needs a big boost to push the country forward.

Haitians are very skilled in designing and making crafts, painting, ethnic dresses, handmade sandals, hats, etc. Haitian crafts have made their way in homes and businesses all over the world due to quality of workmanship, price, meaning, etc. Haitian painting is quite less expensive, but not cheap. You can find quality painting at a very low price.

I remember one time while I was studying at the beach nearby the Jacmelian hotel in Jacmel, a craft merchant who was selling manmade crafts wanted for me to translate for him for a tourist who wanted to buy one of his items. When I told the tourist the price the guy was asking for that item, she could not believe it. She nearly tripled the asking price that the guy wanted for the item. She knew the item was well under-valued. This explains why we need to not only make funds available for those small entrepreneurs, but also we need to make Haiti more appealing to visitors from all over the world.

Tourism plays a very important role in any country's annual revenues. Haiti is a very beautiful island that used to attract a lot of tourists. With the on-going turmoil and lack of security, tourists do not feel secure to vacate in Haiti. Security is very critical in order for Haiti to advance. We have a lot of sites in Haiti that attract a lot of tourists all year around. Haiti is a nice place for vacation all year around. Haiti is a place full of natural beauty for our visitors to see. There are a few things that the minister of tourism should implement to better Haiti and its people:

1. Strive to keep the country clean in collaboration with the private sector.
2. The private sector will do a better job keeping the streets clean.
3. Provide adequate tour/guide for tourists.
4. Provide adequate security for tourists and volunteers
5. Provide a friendly environment for tourists
6. Assist small entrepreneurs to better expose or sell Haitian crafts, paintings, etc.
7. Provide incentives to encourage Haitian investors to invest in the tourist sector, build 4+star hotels, etc.
8. Work with the non-profit sectors like Rotary club and church organizations to work on cleaning projects.
9. Encourage more cruise ships to come to different cities in Haiti
10. Turn "La Gonave" and "La Tortue" islands into a safe haven for tourist with their own security and laws.

CHAPTER 7
Learning to Share

IN ORDER TO CHANGE HAITI, we as Haitians, must be willing to change and learn to give back and make a difference in our homeland. We have to model the way. The game is played inside out. Those in leadership positions have to become role models demonstrating to the average Haitian that they understand the meaning of service. Our leaders need to inspire Haitians inside and outside of Haiti to volunteer more time toward the rebuilding efforts in Haiti. We all see the need to rebuild Haiti. We all want to take action. We all see the need to have a structure in place for everyone to start the odyssey toward rebuilding our country. The words of Wyclef Jean, which follow, provide a guiding light on the important focus of making a difference.

"I have had conversations with gang leaders, met with the police officers and sat down with the leaders of the militias and the army. I have talked with Haitians from all walks of life, all colors of skin, all backgrounds and beliefs. From all these people I hear only one thing in my head and feel only one thing in my heart—that there is only one Haiti. Every Haitian loves their country like a mother loves her child...The objective of

Yéle Haiti is to restore pride and a reason to hope, and for the whole country to regain the deep spirit and force that is part of our heritage." [13]

The Haitian government can learn a great deal from more developed nations. The private sector is very critical to the advancement of any nation. The Haitian government needs to establish a platform for more and more people, Haitians and non-Haitians alike to volunteer to help rebuild the country. In collaboration with the private sector, the government needs to put a structure in place to welcome more volunteers both inside and outside of Haiti. The government needs to create a department in charge of volunteerism. It might be called the *Volunteerism Ministry.*

A volunteer program would stimulate more and more Haitians to take ownership of their country. There is an urgent need to start such a volunteer program and for Haitians to volunteer at least 360 hours or 15 days a year in Haiti. The volunteer minister would administer and coordinate what sector is in dire need such as health care, education, construction, and the like.

In order to create a successful volunteer program, the focus should originate from the very top of Haiti's political power structure. This program will need some tangible coordination, from top to bottom. Haitians need to step up to fix their country. Haitians need to take action or Haiti will remain in its same condition despite of all the millions that have been pledged for assistance. We need capital to rebuild our country, human capital is even more critical at this point. Haitians must do their share to revive Haiti. A volunteer program would include individuals from all ages and from all walks of life. Everyone is included. Haitian people are strong and smart. They can walk wonders if they combine their resources together to save Haiti. Nobody else can do it better than us.

Moreover, the government needs to encourage and facilitate more and more humanitarian assistance that will encourage the Haitian people to become self-reliant. The Haitian people need to be able to feed themselves. We also need to encourage Haitians living abroad to be ambassadors for their country.

Haiti relies too much on foreign aid. We may need foreign aid, but we need to find a systematic way to become more self-reliant. We have some highly capable Haitian technicians and we need to empower them to become more involved in the decision-making process. Indeed, January 12, the anniversary of the earthquake should become an international day for Haiti. Volunteerism needs to be energized in all sectors of the Haitian community, starting with churches, non-governmental organizations, Rotary clubs, Scouts, community organizations, public and private schools, and many others. The community has to come together to save the country.

The private sector also needs to become more involved in investing in the community. The private sector needs to be more supportive of changes that will foster growth and on-going changes. Haitians could soon realize the power of working together while putting our personal interest on the side. Haitians would do wonders as we did prior to 1804, when we defeated France, the strongest Army in the world. We are very intelligent and smart. We need to be more tolerant toward one another. That would help to save the day.

People living abroad could sign up to volunteer their 360 hours in a specific field. The volunteerism minister could create a bi-weekly, monthly, quarterly or yearly calendar of activities for all areas of need. This calendar would have a team in charge to administer all of the support groups. The Haitian government, or the department in charge, would provide shelter and transportation for the volunteers should the need arise. The government would provide adequate security for everyone doing any kind of volunteer work. People could sign up at the beginning of the year or one month ahead of time. The volunteer system would automatically generate a 30-day confirmation to assure complete commitment. There would be a 15-day phone confirmation as a follow-up. The 360-hour program would not be for Haitians only. Any foreigner could sign up to volunteer 360 hours in Haiti in a particular field of expertise.

For projects that are skill-driven, the minister would need to take the process one step farther to minimize waste and mediocrity. The minister would need to validate licenses and expertise in the specific field involved. Failure to do so could be catastrophic for the country. Volunteers must be able to deliver their promises. Trust and confidence are as important as the intention of doing a good job. A concrete road map should be provided to volunteers to follow from day one. Order and professionalism must be maintained in all endeavors. Some areas may not require highly skilled workers. But in certain fields like medicine , renewable or clean energy, road construction, building construction, and many others, we must have qualified individuals in place to execute these projects.

Urgent Need of Medical Care

The needs in the medical field are enormous in all regards. Haiti is in desperate need of physicians to provide care at all levels starting with family practice. Many people who were physically injured in the earthquake constantly need medical care. But not enough medical facilities are available to them, not even the public hospitals. These injured people need on-going assistance. Local Haitian clinics may not have the necessary resources and capital to serve our Haitian brothers and sisters who were left suffering after the earthquake.

More than that many hospitals were severely damaged and need to be rebuilt. Experts are needed to rebuild these hospitals. Unfortunately, the Haitian government and the hospitals may not have the necessary funds available to reconstruct these hospitals. Therefore, the people who are sick or ill cannot find a hospital to accommodate them. It is urgent that we start the rebuilding process.

Most medical assistance is currently being provided through temporary shelters in a condition that is not adequate for the 21st Century. The pain and suffering is unbearable for those who are in need of health care, particularly women with children. We are also in desperate need of surgeons to perform advanced procedures. Many Haitian people cannot afford to go to private hospitals, which are quite expensive. They are forever to live with illness hoping for a miraculous cure or by using natural remedies. Some people are living with growing tumors that need multiple surgeries. They can only pray to God for a miracle to happen.

Haitians are people of strong hope, or "espoir fait vivre," which translate, "with hope there is life." This attitude is deeply rooted in our ability to survive in the most precarious environments. But there remains an urgent need for expert assistance and intervention in the medical field. In order to perform certain surgeries, surgeons need certain equipments, but the hospitals are limited in the medical equipments needed to better serve the Haitian community. To do so, the following steps should be taken.

1. Health service: The Haitian government should rebuild or improve our hospitals' building codes. The government must employ expert support in rebuilding and expanding our hospitals. Our hospitals must meet certain international codes. A hospital building must be able to survive an earthquake of 7.0 magnitudes for a good 60 seconds as well as a category 4 hurricane. Haiti must be rebuilt for the future and any rebuilding effort must call for a stronger building code. Port-au-Prince must revise and improve its building code and make it more stringent. The rebuilding

effort is two-fold. First of all, the government needs to rebuild all of the public hospitals that were damaged or destroyed. This rebuilding effort must be grounded on a stronger foundation. The hospitals must be built with a stronger building code as mentioned before. Second, the new building code must apply to both public and private sectors. The city and other areas need to step up and enforce the building codes.

2. The government, in collaboration with the private sector, also needs to build some new hospitals in response to the medical care needs of the population at large. There now is only one public hospital, "L'hopital General de Port-Au-Prince," in the heart of the capital and people have to drive miles to get there. Even before the earthquake, going to the public hospital with a loved one was a nightmare. At times, this was potentially the worst place to take a patient in need of medical care. Most people who went to the general hospital sick came out sicker. There is an urgent need to build more hospitals in Port-au-Prince, and in other cities, according to a better building code and in an environment more conducive for healing.

3. The leaders in Haiti should establish relationships with some hospitals in the U.S., Canada, France, UK, for different purposes. The first purpose is for advanced training for our physicians. Second, we welcome the opportunity for international hospitals to donate medical equipments to the public hospitals in Haiti. The needs range from beds for patients to surgery equipment and all of the equipment must be labeled and passed through

an on-going inventory to avoid mismanagement. The old pattern cannot be tolerated since it has placed the country in its present condition. The behavior which has caused the tremendous suffering of the Haitian people has to be rooted out. "We can't solve problems by using the same kind of thinking used to create them in the first place,"[14] Albert Einstein once said.

4. The relationship with various foreign donors should extend to the area of training. We need to train Haitian technicians to better use the equipment. Moreover, we also need Haitian technicians to repair the machines in case of operator failure or malfunction. Most of the equipment are computer operated. Therefore, Haitians who are expert in system support are needed to maintain the new equipment.

5. The medical school in Haiti needs to also revise and improve its curriculum to reflect the new improvements in technologies that will be available in some hospitals in Haiti. Additional training will also be needed for physicians to be able to assist their patients. Some of our physicians may have to go to training abroad to polish their skills. We need to continue improving the health care assistance that is being provided to our Haitian brothers and sisters. We have to elevate the medical procedures that we have in place now. And we must improve the hospital facilities to make the environment more conducive to healing those who are in desperate need of care.

The Need for Improvement in Education

One very important step the new government can take is to encourage the private sector to invest in education through the adoption of a public school in Haiti for a period of 10 years or more. Celebrities could be asked to adopt at least one public school in Haiti. And Haitians living abroad could be asked to pool their resources to adopt a school in their homeland. These adoptions could be a full adoption or a half adoption. One way or the other they would benefit the Haitian people as a whole. According to encyclopedia, Wikipedia:

> In 2005, Wyclef Jean established the Yéle Haiti Foundation. In its first year of operation, the foundation, with funding by Comcel (Haitian mobile phone operator that operates a TDMA network in Haiti) provided scholarships to 3,600 children in Gonaïves, Haiti, after the devastation by Hurricane Jeanne. In its second year of operation, it is almost doubling the amount of the scholarships and spreading them throughout Haiti, providing tuition in 5 regions. The foundation aims to provide 6,800 scholarships to children in Port-au-Prince, Gonaïves, Les Cayes, Port-de-Paix, and Cap-Haïtien"[15]

The government in Haiti must think outside of the box. If 100 public schools were adopted or subsidized for a period of 10 years, that would free up the government to build more and better public schools. Of course, the Education Minister will have to establish some clear criteria and guidelines as to how to implement such a school adoption project so that the private sector will indeed have the opportunity to improve the school facilities and learning environment as a whole. Instructors will be paid better and receive more incentives to broaden their teaching horizons and teachers will be held more accountable. They will indeed do a better job in the classroom.

One important observation is that although our Haitian teachers do not receive a decent wage, most do their very best at teaching their students. There are some great Haitian teachers in Haiti. That's why most Haitian students are well prepared when they come to the United States or any foreign countries to study. Teachers always do their very best whether they get paid on time or not. Sometimes, six months may go by without a paycheck, and they still come to teach each day. And they still have to take care of their own families. All of these things can be resolved if we put our resources together and prepare the way for our Haitian brothers and sisters to have a better tomorrow.

We must take care of our country. Creating such a school adoption program will improve the lives of our Haitian brothers and sisters if all of the indicators are put in place and constantly monitored by a highly skilled team. Too much "laissez-faire" will take us back to where we are today. There is no longer room for any mistakes or trial and error. There also is no room for any backdoor deals. We must take charge for a better Haiti and its people.

The various ministries in Haiti must have branches in other countries where they are a lot of Haitians like The United States, Canada and France. The goal is to inspire Haitians of all ages to support their country. We need for Haitians to solve the problems of their own country. Who can do it better than we can? As a matter of fact, it is our country. We must bring it back on its feet again; otherwise, Haiti will vanish before our eyes. Let's not blame others. Let's roll up our sleeves and get to work. We have a brain like everyone else. We have done a lot when we put our heads together. Let's get to it and do it.

CHAPTER 8
Learning to Serve with Six Sigma

HAITI'S ELECTED OFFICIALS NEED TO activate some systematic problem solving measures to put the country back on track. Most important, there must be a mentality shift in the way we not only treat our country, but also in the way we treat one another. Some elected officials from the president to the rural police have no plan to assist the community at large. Their main focus is to help themselves and their immediate families. Our elected officials need to be held more accountable in the way they meet the community's expectations.

The mentality of some elected officials in Haiti is directly pointed to two things: power and money. In many cases, our elected officials are not held accountable by the people and their superiors. Once they hold their position, they forget about the needs of the majority. Of course, they are now in power. Once they are in power, who can dare talk to them? They only see their time for the opportunity to have a nice car, a nice house, women left and right, and travel abroad. They could care less about the community in which they live. The worst thing is that they may build a beautiful home in the suburbs, but they will not pave the road that leads to their home. They would rather steer four-wheel drive.

The on-going image is that helping the average Haitian family is the last thing on the agenda or in the mind of these elected officials. Often when you go to their offices, the people there are not willing to help you. They would rather take your head off, especially if you cannot say a few French words or you look uneducated. If you try to force yourself in, they will make fun of you. Most elected officials do not go to work on time. When they do get to work, they would rather talk with their peers or leave the office to go visit friends and family members, or go shopping. The service at the government offices has always been poor or below average.

The Haitian governmental staff will definitely need some logistical support to come up with a durable solution to Haiti's everlasting and unreliable services. It would be very practical for Haiti's elected officials to receive Six-Sigma Problem Solving training, particularly the senators, congressmen and women, governors, police officers, judges, directors, managers and the like, and to teach them systematic problem solving and re-engineering skills. The most important aspect of Wyclef Jean's leadership will be his ability to bring international influence to Haiti. He will need to create a bridge between the elected officials who are part of Haiti's core decision making team, and the international community in order to remove the "hit-and-run" aid request attitude toward the international community. We need to continue working with the international community with an open mind to bettering our country. Let's find a systematic way to keep the back and side doors closed and prevent elected officials from seeking financial assistance pretended for Haiti and not used to enrich themselves without being held accountable for their wrong doing.

My assessment of Haitian government officials is based on a true story that I, Jacques Guillaume, witnessed when I was in Haiti in 1994. The house of a close friend's mother's was nearly burned down. In the process of trying to put out the fire, her mother suffered second degree burns over much of her body. She was rushed to the public hospital, L'hopital General de Port-au-Prince from Jacmel because the hospital there is better equipped to handle this kind of trauma. Three days later, I went to the hospital to see my friend's mother. That was my first time entering the general hospital. When I walked in the hospital, I saw someone with blood all over lying on the concrete inside of the hospital at the mercy of his family. It looked like he had been hit by a car or fallen at a construction site. I called a nurse to bring that to her attention. She told me the doctor had not yet come in. I said to her, "Can you at least give him some preliminary first aid care?"

The nurse's response was, "Is the injured person your relative?"

My response was, "What difference does that make?"

The nurse then told me to mind my own business because Doctor Vincent was supposed to be in about three hours earlier and had yet to show up if he was even coming in at all. The nurse informed me that she was "just the meat" between the two layers of the sandwich. She was trying her best.

Then I continued on to see my friend's mother. When I walked in, she was in a tiny room with four other patients with unrelated illnesses. My heart was torn in pieces. I asked my friend if the doctor had seen her mother. She told me the doctor had come only once, about two days ago.

Of course, her mother needed urgent care. So I read her chart to find out who the doctor was. My friend and I went on a search to track the doctor down in the maze of the hospital. The conditions in which patients were being treated through all of the walk-ways were inhuman. When we finally reached the doctor's office, he was not in yet and no one knew what time he was coming in.

I asked another physician to come take a look at the patient for me because her health was becoming more precarious by the minute. He promised that he would come as soon as he was done with the patient he was with.

Of course, people get sicker when they go to the hospital if they do not receive immediate care. When the physician showed up, he was also shocked to see the burned condition of my friend's mother, which should have received immediate attention from day one. He gave a long prescription list to the family. When a family in Haiti goes to the hospital, they are responsible for bringing everything such as tape, gauze, pads, IVs, etc. The family in this case did their very best to purchase the requested prescriptions although they were not prepared for this kind of emergency. The care also was provided a little too late. The lady lost her life due to the hospital's negligence. This is very common at the public hospital. That's why most Haitian people would rather go to a private hospital if they can afford it. The physicians are more reliable at a private hospital.

Stories like this are endless in a country out of control, where politicians and government officials want to keep outside "checks and balances" away from Haiti's government chaos. They do not want anyone outside their sphere of influence to point out the corruption and lack of basic care for the average Haitian.

SECTION IV:
WELCOME TO OUR WORLD

CHAPTER 9
Our Country

WYCLEF JEAN WRAPS HIMSELF IN the Haitian flag as if he and Haiti were one. Haiti is at the very core of Wyclef Jean's presence and forms the foundation of his existence. The love of Jean for his homeland has been shown to be firm and abundant. The affection and love for his people is not a timid response to win an election. Jean has sought to help his people when helping was not very popular. It was a matter of duty and obligation to go back to his homeland and help out time and time again. It was this devotion that Haiti's current president, René Préval, recognized in naming Jean Haiti's ambassador to the world.

What an awesome difference it would make if many of the people from our homeland, who have achieved greatness in many parts of the world, would come out and boldly identify themselves as Haitians. Many of my countrymen have achieved greatness in the United States and other countries attributing any of their success to the culture and beautiful people of their homeland.

We are a great black nation, the first to rebel against tyranny to fight and gain our independence. We are forever a great people who have suffered, but through it all we have maintained a great sense of dignity and have a great deal to give back.

The poor and the average Haitian search dearly for life in any avenue possible. They are left to carry the baggage of identity on their shoulders and continue to bear the burden of some of the negative connotations associated with our people in the past.

Shame on me and shame on the many who have distanced ourselves from the misery and despair of our homeland. We have abandoned our little island and now can only glance at the misery from afar allowing the politicians to do as they wish. We seem to have concluded that the rule of law has forever escaped the consciousness of the politicians of our homeland.

The main goal of Haiti's ruling class seems to be to maintain the status quo and allow the rest of the country to live in misery and despair, as if the entire scenario is unseen. The idea seems to be to maintain control and prevent those who have left from ever being able to contribute politically to the country. If you found success and a better life somewhere else, you are forever barred from the political process in Haiti or contributing to the country's government in any way.

> Wyclef Jean told Voice of America (VOA) he is appealing to Haiti's government to address a number of concerns about the approval process used by election officials, who authorized 19 candidates for the presidential vote. He said candidates who have lived outside Haiti were mostly excluded by the Provisional Electoral Council (CEP). "It looked like every other candidate that was out was a diaspora candidate and that is a form of prejudice on the CEP's part," Wyclef Jean said.

> As part of his election campaign, Wyclef Jean had hoped to reform the relationship between Haiti and the hundreds of thousands of Haitians who have fled the country. He said, that if elected, he hoped to change the constitution to remove a ban on dual citizenship and offer many Haitians abroad a chance to vote in elections.
>
> Many Haitians rely on money from family members abroad, who send back more than $1.5 billion a year. But Haitians outside the country say residency requirements and other laws can limit their legal rights in their home country.[16]

A system has been created where many of us, in spite of our very achievements all over the world, can no longer go back to our homeland to make a difference. We are guided by our Haitian values and culture, but we can only view our country from afar and are unable to make a difference in our homeland. This is a system completely different from that of many developed nations, who understand that those who have gained knowledge abroad should be welcomed back by the political process to contribute and make their country better.

The sound must be heard loud and clear that Haiti is our home, and demand a better government from the heavy handed politicians who believe that the one percent who now control Haiti should forever remain in power. "Although the Provisional Electoral Council (CEP's) deliberations should be largely technical, critics say they have become subject to political manipulation by a Haitian political elite seeking to limit the participation of powerful Haitians living abroad."[17]

The politicians and their need to control have taken away our rights to our homeland. We have agreed to masquerade ourselves and accept the concept that we are no longer Haitians and are no longer fit to participate in the future of the people in our homeland. But we are forever Haitian and have looked Haitian from the very start. Those who are left in control in Haiti should now create a more open system and allow the people of Haiti to profit from all that we have learned abroad.

Every developed country has seen its citizens learn and grow abroad and has welcomed them back to contribute to the betterment of their homeland. Why have a system where a ruling one percent drains everything for its sole benefit and has no concern for the well-being of the masses.

I ask the good Lord, our Father in heaven, what is it that makes our leaders so cold to the plight of the masses of Haitians, my fellow brothers, and allows them to suffer in poverty of the worst kind. It is as if our leaders are maintaining the people of Haiti in a cage, staring slowly in the face of the world. I do not know why our leaders are so cold and abusive. In a way I must cry because maybe I am the same. Maybe I would do the same if I were a Haitian in power. Maybe I would allow the masses to starve and only think of myself. What is God? What are we as Haitians? Why are our leaders so cold and brutal? I cry because I know deep inside that this system may never change.

Why have I been allowed to escape from living in the greatest country in the world? A country full of hope, a country with the courage to do what is right? I remember when the United States had a chance to elect Barack Obama and I felt in my heart the greatness of his leadership. And I thank God for being a Haitian-American and I feel honored for having helped to elect Barack Obama as our President. This man is by far the greatest man I have ever had a chance to lay my eyes on. If I died tomorrow, my life would have been worth every breath for having cast my vote and having had the privilege to witness this man's presidency.

What about the Haitian millionaire, Wyclef Jean? What it is about this great musician who despite all his achievements, he remains Haitian at the very core. The man has everything and is also a musician of the highest order. He has worked with the greatest musician of our times. Why sacrifice him among a leadership class that shows no respect for life and could possibly harm him without the slight hesitation? Somehow the people know that he cares. They immediately identify him as one of their own. This individual is their fellow countryman.

CHAPTER 10
Preserving the Land

As a land owner in Haiti, I usually use Google Earth Web site to look around any new developments in Haiti, and particularly in Jacmel. The view of the capital of Haiti, Port-au-Prince is disheartening. The degradation of our land could be seen from miles away even before the earthquake of January 12, 2010. If you zoomed the entire island from Google Earth, the sharp contrast of greenery is very noticeable between Haiti and the Dominican Republic.

Obviously, the deforestation did not occur over night. It has been a legacy of deforestation that our leaders chose to ignore even after mudslides that killed so many in Gonaives. Haitian farmers have been cutting trees down as a means to respond to their family obligations. As we are all aware, it is urgent that such a legacy be reversed to improve the lives in this fragile island, which used to be a "pearl island."

According to Dr. Thomas B. Byers, Director of the Commonwealth Center for Humanities and Society at the University of Louisville, the contrast in Haiti's landscape versus Dominican Republic next door can be described in Christopher Columbus' own words. On Dec. 13, 1492,

Columbus described his first view of Haiti as follows: "All the trees were green and full of fruit and the plants tall and covered with flowers. The roads were broad and good. The climate was like April in Castile; the nightingale and other birds sang as they do in Spain during the month, and it was the most pleasant place in the world."[18]

To better preserve Haiti a long-term and feasible agriculture and infrastructure plan must be actuated by different groups from the private sector, by the farming association, and by a non-governmental body in collaboration with the USAID. The words of Wyclef Jean clearly define the needed steps to make a difference in Haiti.

> "In Haiti now, there aren't enough crops harvested to feed even one-third of the country, and the island's tree cover is practically nonexistent — less than 2 percent. I'm telling you, you probably can't envision what that means.

> "We need adequate tree coverage to help shield the island from the worst damages that can be caused by the storms that rage throughout the year, and to help block soil erosion, which the rainy season (we're in the midst of it right now) makes much worse. In turn, excessive soil erosion further degrades farming conditions, making it a factor in the country's inability to grow enough food to feed the population.

> "On another stop on our recent trip, my wife, Claudinette, was happy to give a $10,000 check to an agricultural community center in the mountains. These community farmers harvest most of the vegetables bought and sold in Haiti, and we want to help make sure they can continue to do that. We also conducted a tree-planting ceremony to kick off

Yéle Vert, the forestation program that the clothing company Timberland is co-sponsoring with us."[19]

Since I grew up in Haiti, I can describe in details the true character of a Haitian and our strong farming heritage. I will start with my parents. I was raised by two hard working people with strong family values and respect for God. My dad is a deacon in a small Catholic church in a small town in the countryside. Every Sunday we would go to church rain or shine. That's why my mom still has the nickname "Madam Legliz" which in Creole means Mrs. Church.

My dad raised us to be strong and mindful of our character. He strongly believes in hardworking people. He always refers to the bible to support his point. My dad was always the first one out of bed and the last one to go to bed. He is a typical hardworking Haitian. He is also a farmer. He does farming, lumbering, animal farming, and is also a community activist. My mom is also a farmer supporting my dad and a small retail food vendor. My dad always goes to work early in the morning and he always carries his "pickwa" shovel to work. When he starts working, the early morning rain gives him his first shower. At noon, he is still working under the sun and his sweat gives him another shower.

My Father strongly believes that "you earn your daily bread with the sweat from your forehead." His most common crops are corn, black or red beans and potatoes. My dad does all kind of jobs to support his family. The other side of his farming job is to sell fruit like mangoes, watermelons, nectarines, bananas, and the like. My dad used to farm a lot of nectarine, grapefruit, and oranges during the fruit season.

In addition to being a farmer, my father is a lumberjack. Whenever the farming season is over or during a bad farming season, he used to travel miles and miles to do lumber jobs. He also raised his own trees. My dad always made enough money treating lumber to feed his family. But he is always against deforestation and holds seminars to teach people how to plant trees, and especially the kinds of trees that are critical for the environment. He always teaches other people in our area to wait for a tree to mature before selling it.

Moreover, my dad and my mom raised animals like turkeys, pigs, goats, cows, horses, donkeys, and the like. My dad became a veterinarian by practice. People from miles away used to bring their animals to my dad for treatment. My dad does castration for most animals ranging from dogs to mules. When anyone comes to our home, they can see all kinds of animals. We had hens and roosters, turkeys, turtle doves, pigeons, rabbits, and the like. My mother believed every child should have at least three hens and/or roosters and goats. Since my mom and my dad had six of us, all boys, everyone had a lot of hens and roosters and goats.

It is sad to say that the Haitian government is not equipped, and cannot be trusted, to deliver a land renewal project of such magnitude. The greenery and the clean rivers of Haiti did not disappear overnight, and there must be a long-term, viable restoration plan to foster ongoing prosperity. To promote a more sustainable agricultural endeavor, the following must be done.

- Investment in land development and reclaiming of unused land is a must. As reported by the United States Agency for International Development (USAID), agricultural development has always been and is a proven engine of growth that alleviates global hunger and reduces poverty. Moreover, the past centuries have proven that agricultural growth is a key factor in industrial growth and economic development in England, United States, Japan, and modern China. Food is very critical to any developed nation and especially to a non-developed country with close to 10 million people like Haiti.

• A strong land restoration and agricultural project must be set forth to better Haiti. This long-term project must extend for at least 10 to 20 years to cover all of the cities and rural areas of Haiti. One of the goals of this project is land restoration. For land that is unused and unable to produce crops, the owners or landlords will lease these properties out to the organization for a period of 10 to 20 years for a reasonable annual fee. All of these properties will be fenced to provide a better picture of each pilot program. Fencing of hundreds of acres of land will in turn create a lot of jobs for the people living in the rural areas.

• There is an urgent need to set a path for the landlords, or teams of landlords and farmers to participate proactively in this land restoration project. There will be small groups of landlords or farmers who will be working together to assure that the project delivers as promised. They will also be held accountable for working with various teams from different levels to carry out other special projects. Of course, all of the structure will have to be in place to prevent waste and prevent abuse from people filling up their pockets. The land will have to be cleared and prepared first. Furthermore, there will be a need to spray the land with fertilizer to make it ready for plants to grow.

• Another crucial step is soil erosion prevention. The first step is to plant a lot of trees that will systematically prevent erosion or landslides.

Planting trees will definitely help restore the loss of our most urgent needs like water. Most of the trees planted will be oaks, which will be planted 15 square feet apart. There will be approximately 450 oak trees per acre of land. Planting these trees will also create jobs for people living in the area.

- In addition to planting trees, the land will also be cultivated in a way to stop soil erosion. Fruit trees will be planted along with the oak trees and should be tropical in nature like nectarines, oranges, lemons, and the like. All of this will be better for the people living in the area. At each land restoration project location there will be at least one water retention cistern that can retain millions of gallons of water when it rains. The rainwater will in turn be used to water crops should there not be any river nearby. Water will also be used as a means to spray fertilizer on the crops.

- Good farming methods are a must in Haiti. The plantations should vary with corn, beans, rice, fruit, bananas, plantains and vegetables. Some plants like corn, beans, and vegetables can be cultivated twice a year. Fruits and rice may be cultivated once a year. Corn will be planted everywhere on these properties. Corn is more flexible and can grow almost anywhere as long as the land is clear and ready for use. Beans, bananas and plantains need more water to grow. Beans are very sensitive to the heat and should be planted in selective areas where there is a lot of shade. Vegetables also need shade and water. There will also be a need to create some greenhouse projects to grow fruit and vegetables throughout the entire year. Growing natural food will surely be a good path for Haitian farmers. Each farming group will be required to follow up on these projects and report back to the team in charge.

- Agribusiness is vital. Teams of farmers, landlords and non-land owners will work together to pick up crops. A process will be set forth to pick up and deliver crops to designated locations. Half of the crops collected will be donated to people living and working in the land restoration project areas, i.e. farmers, landlords and other individuals. The other half will be sold to Haitian wholesalers to generate funds to acquire more land and to fund other projects. All of these crops will be sold on the local or national market at a fixed markup rate in order to keep the food price low.

- The surplus of corn and bananas may be used to create cornflakes for example, which will foster an industry of food transformation. All of this will definitely promote a robust Haitian agribusiness system to significantly and effectively restore the environment and create employment, growth and prosperity.

These ideas, if followed effectively, will assure the ability of self-reliance within 10 years. For this project to be implemented effectively, cheap imports of subsidized produce from the U.S. must be barred from entering the Haitian market. This kind of dumping of goods, like rice on the local market drove Haitian farmers off their land since they were unable to compete. These are the kinds of projects we expect a president like Wyclef Jean to foster. Agricultural restoration has become a must. It is unacceptable for Haiti to lose close to 99 percent of its forests in the 21st Century.

CHAPTER 11
Haiti Cherie

HOW MANY PUBLIC FIGURES LIVING abroad are Haitians, or have a Haitian background, but have hidden this fact from the world? How many of our people do not see the benefit of proclaiming their Haitian ancestry? But there is a man who stood tall when it was not bold and fancy to proclaim oneself to be Haitian. There is a man who wrapped himself in the Haitian flag as if he and the flag were one.

Wyclef Jean did not have to take a leap of faith. Embracing his homeland, the island of Hispaniola, seemed like a natural reaction, like embracing his mother. Wyclef Jean and the love for his homeland is a natural phenomenon. Wyclef Jean is like the pearl of our adopted land, our President Barack Obama, a man of honor and godliness. President Obama gave up the possibility of a life of luxury to serve the less fortunate and God rewarded him abundantly. These acts of greatness by Obama resemble those of our own Wyclef Jean and his love for Haiti and its people, and his willingness to take a chance of being rejected in order to embrace Haiti more fully.

There are certain qualities in life that one cannot learn overnight and sometimes you may not be able to learn them at all. To love one's homeland with the deepest love is something intrinsic that one cannot masquerade. It comes with love in a higher sense and pursuing a higher cause in the hope of making a difference in the world. This cannot be learned by leaders overnight. These grand ideas have to be part of one's character, formatted in the formative years with the knowledge of looking out for the less fortunate. As the son a preacher, Wyclef Jean says, "I have asked the Haitian people on the ground of course is going to be suffering, frustrated, violence, I tell them that I do not cry for myself. I cry for them."[20] The words of Wyclef Jean's ideas are not accidental. They are ingrained with the love of other and of higher causes, no matter what obstacle or challenges life may throw in his way.

What is the meaning of Wyclef Jean's deepest love for Haiti? Why has he embraced his heritage when taking such a leap of faith could have been fatal to his career? Why must everything depend on the life of being accepted not only as a great musician, but also as a great Haitian? Some may say Wyclef Jean's actions were those of a man accustomed to loving his people and the country of his birth. The fact remains that no matter what may be the justification may be for his action, it is crystal clear that he has forever changed the meaning of being Haitian. The fight and struggle for our homeland, in the eyes of Wyclef Jean, is a cry of deepest love. It is a cry emboldened by the love and honor of being identified with a struggle encircled with pain, suffering and all of the challenges for a better tomorrow. Wyclef Jean reminds us in his own words:

> "There's the near future, in which we need to continue to provide as much support and aid as possible to the people still living in tents (about 1.2 million at last count), those living on the streets and those living in the rubble of their homes. They all lack adequate water supplies, enough food, a sense of security."

Wyclef Jean added, "Five-and-a-half years ago, I co-founded Yéle Haiti, a non-governmental organization that supports the country's educational programs, as well as the Jean et Marie Orphanage, which houses, feeds, clothes and educates its children. On our last visit to Haiti, we gave care packages to the 57 orphans who live there."

He continued to say, "The young people also need physical education to help them take their minds off these difficult times. Yéle sponsors L'Athlétique d'Haïti, an after-school program that plans activities for 650 kids and gives them a safe place to go instead of hanging out and getting into trouble — or worse, being at risk for becoming a victim of the crime and violence that's everywhere in Haiti. On Yéle's recent trip, "we presented the program with a $10,000 check to keep up its great work, and we gave the kids cleats, water bottles and jerseys. But, man, you should have seen their smiles when the guest we brought to meet them, French national soccer star Florent Malouda, said he'd play futbol with them."

Moreover Wyclef Jean mentioned, "As happy as we were to see them so carefree, it was also a reminder that our efforts aren't enough. It's so important to Haiti's long-term recovery and rebuilding that more NGOs, businesses, government agencies and individuals take up the cause of restructuring the education system so that we can give Haiti's youngest generations the tools they need — and deserve — to be productive, innovative participants in the Haiti of the future."[21]

Wyclef Jean reminds us that the fight is not over. The concept of appreciating our homeland is truly important for survival and growth as a people and as a nation. What does it mean to love Haiti? Some say if you don't love yourself and your own identity, then you cannot love others. The facts are that as Haitians, many of us do not speak of our heritage in daylight. There are some Haitians, even today, living in many places around the world, who hide their Haitian heritage as if it were a bad plague. In their minds, disclosing their Haitian heritage would have a negative influence on their lives. They must conceal their true identify or somehow feel a sense of degradation.

There are some who have achieved fame but hide their Haitian individuality from the public. Why would someone want to hide the foundation of his or her belief? There was a time when proclaiming one's Haitian background would be scorned or looked upon with some sort of stare. Sadly, Haiti, the first free black republic in the Western Hemisphere has turned into a center of destruction and despair.

As a teenager living in the city of Miami, I remember being part of an incident which does not provide good comfort to my memory. I remember accompanying by my brother Stanley and my father to a shoe store to purchase some footwear. The store clerks were two Spanish gentlemen with a rather disparaging outlook toward Haitians. In those days, Miami was dominated by those of Hispanic heritage and we, as Haitians controlled almost no major stores of our own, unlike today. I remember speaking English with my younger brother, masking as Americans with our newfound language.

There was a man of possible Haitian ancestry shopping in the same store. The store clerk and his friends discovered a perfect opportunity to belittle the pitiable shopper. They begin to talk among themselves, laughing out loud and finally asked the shopper the uncomfortable question, "Are you Haitian?" They asked the question in mocking voices speaking English with their presumably Creole ascent. Then they joked among themselves when the man was reluctant to respond.

The quiet shopper pretended not to hear the question and continued to shop.

"Hey," the storekeeper blurted out as if he had spotted a burglary suspect or something completely repugnant about the patron. The shopper had no option but to turn his glance toward the store clerks. "Are you Haitian?" The question came out loud and clear.

The shopper was silent for a moment and then in distaste began to walk out of the store while muttering his response, "Me, me no Haitian." From the man's voice, being familiar with the Haitian accent, I concluded that he probably was Haitian, ashamed and disgusted.

The store clerk and his partner carried on as if it was more important to get a cheap laugh from the man, than focusing on their business needs. My brother and I, being only teenagers, joined in their laughter while pretending that we had escaped our own ancestry. We were overjoyed mistakenly in believing that we were off the hook because in our minds we were young Americans speaking English without an accent. In reality, however, we were wrong in thinking that we had camouflaged our ancestry and somehow escaped from ourselves. We were highly mistaken because even today, having lived in this country for over 20 years, my accent is crystal clear and always definable as that of a Haitian. And I am extremely proud of who I am.

As an adult, I've realized that we as Haitians should be proud of our heritage. We are a people born of fire who are always achieving and coming out on top through amazing challenges. We are extraordinary people, with remarkable accomplishments. The problem is that many of us have lost our identity. We have hidden ourselves in our small circles and no longer want to be connected with a history of challenges and abuse of our leaders. Many of us have given up on the island, knowing that in the near future many will die and the poor will forever remain poor, the weak will forever remain weak, and the tiny ruling class of one percent will continue to abuse their power and walk on the people as if they did not exist.

The fact that our own Wyclef Jean will not be president in the near future is indisputable. We know that most likely whoever becomes president will not wrap him in the Haitian flag, or forever intertwine his love of our homeland and our people. No matter the outcome, we are Haitians forever in spite of the suffering and pain. The words of Wyclef Jean should give us comfort: "I was inspired to run for president because I know Haiti can become great with the right leadership."[22]

No matter what the outcome of the election in Haiti, we must not walk away from our homeland. We are a great people with the ability to accomplish great things. We must not shy away from our ability to pursue greatness and make a great difference in Haiti. We must search deep inside and learn to love and respect each other. We must be proud and with the fullness of our breath, we must proclaim loud and clear from the mountain top that we are Haitian and Haiti is our love.

SECTION V:
THE INVISIBLE ONES

CHAPTER 12
The Silent Majority

IN A WAY, THE CATASTROPHE which struck Haiti on January 12, 2010 is inconceivable, and the destruction that it brought is unimaginable. The immediate conclusion could be that Haiti is in a position where the possibility for greatness is forever gone. Some could walk through the rubble and take their hats off while looking at the misery and suffering and miss the opportunity that awakes in the midst of this disaster. In effect, a closer look at what happened because of the disaster which struck Haiti may show signs of an extraordinary opportunity.

The earthquake is an unwanted disaster of the worst proportion, but there lies within it the creation of a society where the majority of Haitians now find themselves together as one people. The poor, the rich, the mulattos, and the government elite have all suffered and become one in some sense, living in tents with the hope of finding a good outcome.

There now is a chance for a great awakening as a result of this misery and pain for the people of Haiti, but a final chance for the Haitian people as a whole to have a common journey. Can this journey be realized with the realization that all Haitians deserve a chance for a better life? This important concept forces an evaluation of this disaster through a different prism, allowing a broader perspective and realizing the opportunity to remake this nation. Is this a final chance for 99 percent of Haitians suffering from the bottom to finally have a chance to be part of the process for a successful nation?

Haitians today find themselves in a country where the tragedy has touched all, and only working together as one people can a better society be created. This is once in a life time opportunity. The chance to create a nation of one people, where all Haitians have finally gotten a chance to contribute and benefit from their island, has finally arrived. The country can finally be built from the bottom up, where the downtrodden, the poor living invisible lives and the ruling class can all be part of the process as one Haitian family. This is finally a chance to create a society, which recognizes all individuals with the right to live a free and fruitful life.

The opportunity brought on by this terrible disaster can only be understood by going back through time and looking at it through the lens of history. There is a need to look through history and analyze the timeline, which bought us to this day, where a nation of black African slaves, brought to life by "Jean-Jacques Dessalines, was born as a slave and later became a leader of the Haitian Revolution."[23]

The history of this truly remarkable man highlights the very nature of Haitian society. "Haiti is the world's oldest black republic and one of the oldest republics in the Western Hemisphere. Although Haiti actively assisted the independence movements of many Latin American countries— and secured a promise from the great liberator, Simon Bolívar, that he would free their slaves after winning independence from Spain— the nation of former slaves was excluded from the hemisphere's first regional meeting of independent nations, held in Panama in 1826."[24] The newly formed Republic of Haiti, who had helped other nations to find their freedom, excluded, always having this mark of blackness forcing it to suffer in the worst possible ways.

On January 1, 1804, the people of Haiti decided to challenge General Napoleon and face the great army of France and gain their independence, becoming the first black nation of free men, and the second nation declaring itself a free republic on this side of the Atlantic after the United States. "On January 1, 1804 Dessalines then declared independence, reclaiming the indigenous Taine name of Haiti ("Land of Mountains") for the new nation. Most of the remaining French colonists fled ahead of the defeated French army." [25] This bold move would not come without consequences, however.

Haiti was isolated for 80 years with the inability to trade with most nations. The little island was left to fend for itself, unacceptable to the society of on the nations. Internally, a caste system was created, where the lighter skinned mulattos would gain control of the country with their lighter skins as proof of their superiority. In time the darker skinned majority, consisting of most of the population, was left to a life of permanent suffering.

Creole Is Understood

Little has changed over the years. Haiti is still run by invisible people speaking French on special occasions to impress the public. The majority of Haitians suffer through the rubble while speaking Haitian Creole and dropping a French sentence here and there to elevate their status, like drops of rain falling on the ocean. The ability to define their status, from time to time, with their ability to speak French is little but an annoying fact. The majority of people in Haiti suffer while speaking Creole. They are the poor with the inability to change their status. They are trapped with a language of their homeland defining themselves as Haitians undeserving of a good life.

The opportunity that faces us now is a country completely

destroyed and where both poor and rich finds themselves on the street living among each other as one Haitian people struggling to find life in the rains. The key to change lies in giving the majority of Haitians a voice. The ninety nine percent of Haitians have to become part of the process. Creole has to be given a place at the table, and the majority of Haitians can no longer be excluded.

The people who assumed greatness used French words, which often contained no substance to make a difference in the life of the average Haitians. The true fact is that nothing has changed in Haiti. The rubble will remain, the streets will forever be the same, and there is no one to blame but the one percent and their dominance and selfishness in trading the life of the people in exchange for power and control.

Wyclef Jean is a man of the people, who realizes that those at the bottom with their Creole, their pain and their suffering are Haitians just like he is the son of a preacher who realizes that God has created all man equal and deserving of a chance to a good life. All Haitians deserve a life just as grand as those who have dominated the political culture. Creole should not be a barrier, but a badge of honor to hold and carry as a true sign of true of our African ancestry.

Wyclef Jean has violated the unwritten law. He speaks Creole in daylight and only Creole. The ability to speak Creole boldly is troubling to the elite. In Wyclef Jean there is no masquerade, no hidden agenda, and no pretension on dropping a French line here and there. The transparency of Wyclef Jean is too much to bear. If one would truly evaluate the conditions in Haiti, then one would see that the very change that Haiti needs lies in Wyclef Jean. The poor have to be given a voice and be made part of the process. Haiti cannot survive by being ruled by the upper class with little regard for the average Haitians.

Let Creole be spoken in every corner of Haiti, loud and clear. The proud voice of the people cannot be silent. The majority of Haitians have to be allowed to speak. They have to be given a voice and their well-being has to be part of the process. If the political process in Haiti takes the same path it has and the majority of Haitians are not allowed to speak up, the contest is once again controlled by the elite and the well-being of the average Haitian is dismissed as unimportant. Nothing will change. May God help us. Please be mindful of the Haitian people.

The suffering and pain of the Haitian people reminds me of my childhood living on this beautiful island and swimming in a little ravine in **Grand Goâve,** surrounded by flowers. This was paradise. The country was grand and so were the people, the common Haitians with their kindness and their willingness to give and share their best with a friend or neighbor. In my world this was a time of innocence.

Some of my parents' extended family and friends were of the privileged class. I, Jean-Max Jocelyn remember being told, upon visiting the homes of the elite that their children were only allowed to speak French. Upon being introduced, I was always silent, like a creature from outer space, while their children played like little birds flying free and in control of their surroundings. It is as if they were noble and special.

In my world, with only the ability to speak Creole, French was the language of the gods and the French ruled us like slaves. I was a common Haitian, with only the ability to speak Creole. I was to remain forever and unworthy as I sat there and listen to the children of the elite speaking French. They were like angels whom I somehow must forever serve. I was part of the silent majority, stuck until I became of age and could obtain an education and learn to speak French. It was the unfulfilled hope of every Haitian to speak French and become part of the accepted class of Haitians, destined to survive and live a decent life in Haiti.

Today, as an adult, in no way do I ever, ever care to speak French. Like Wyclef Jean, I'm Haitian. Creole is spoken and

Creole is understood. And forever I will speak Creole. I no longer see it as a cardinal sin to speak the language of my birth. I no longer look at those who speak French as something special. The average Haitian is special. The change in Haiti will occur when common Haitians, speaking Creole in the light of the day and speaking words of truth truly make a difference in the lives of the people.

There is no greater injustice, and no greater abuse of the people of Haiti, then preventing Wyclef Jean or someone like him from being part of the political process. The very notion which has excluded him will also exclude the majority of Haitians from all of the benefits of their island. Any excuse to exclude a statesman like Wyclef Jean is a tragedy of the greatest proportion. The fact is the ruling class in Haiti will continue to have no shame while Haiti remains in a deplorable condition. Why would the elite exclude someone who could shine a bright light on the island? Why would the elite prevent the world from looking at Haiti with its beautiful people? The ruling class will stop at nothing, not even the well-being of the Haitian people.

If only somehow, we could empower Wyclef Jean and allow him to become the voice of the average Haitian and Creole be spoken loud and clear in the midst of those who have held Haiti hostage. Then Haiti could gain center stage in the affairs of the world at large. Haitians deserve nothing less than transformation and Wyclef Jean can help make it happen.

CHAPTER 13
Yes, We Can!

How beautiful is the history of the island of Hispaniola? Haiti, as the first nation of African descent to have gained its independence, is truly noteworthy. The Haitian people through very challenging circumstances revolted against slavery and gained their right to govern themselves. Their heroic efforts and success influence the world on a path toward common freedom for all mankind.

Richard A. Haggerty wrote in the article titled, *Haiti: A Country Study,* "When it secured its independence from France, Haiti moved to the forefront of political history. The Haitian Revolution took place at the same period as the American and the French revolutions, and Haiti was one of the first nations to abolish slavery."[26] The influence of Haiti toward the freedom of all mankind is unquestionable.

The logical conclusion is that the heroic effort of the African descendants in Haiti had a major impact on the African slaves living in the United States. Haitians having fought France, a superpower at the time, and becoming victorious is truly a fight of great proportion. The people of the United States must have known of this history and been influenced by such a heroic fight. In the article written in Wikipedia by Samuel M. Wilson titled, *Hispaniola: Caribbean chiefdoms in the age of Columbus*, "Haiti is the only nation born of a slave revolt. Haiti's perseverance and successful resistance against colonial forces would influence the future of the United States Civil War."[27]

It is unfortunate, that after gaining the freedom to rule ourselves, we became mired in a struggle by leaders who could not find an interest greater than their own. Our leaders have chosen to serve their own interests at the expense of their countrymen while Haiti has been mired forever by some internal struggle. Our little island has paid the terrible price of existing in a state of suffering and pain for its citizens.

No one would have believed that, as African descendants that we would have subjugated our people to similar conditions of abuse and tyranny. Nothing can be compared with slavery, but the conditions created by our abusive leaders have slowly lowered the country into a state of oppression. The island eventually fell to the very bottom with the unwelcome distinction of being the poorest country in the western hemisphere, a situation created by leaders who have chosen to enrich themselves at the expense of the majority of Haitians. Our government mostly operates for its own benefit and the people have become tools to be used to increase the wealth and status of individuals in the highest positions.

As stated by Richard A. Haggerty, "Most Haitians viewed government functionaries as beneficiaries of patronage and the spoils system rather than as public servants. The state traditionally supported and maintained the established political order and extracted wealth from the population. Citizens therefore expected little or nothing from government. Rather, they saw the state as an entity that confiscated, taxed, prohibited, or imprisoned."[28]

The majority of Haitians have little choice but to endure under a system, where the rule of law or the benefit of the people is not within the psyche of those in power. The arrangement seems to be set by a group which believes that government serves only to extract as much from the people as possible. Donations and goods from foreign sources are treated like funds from some illegal source and millions of dollars in contributions disappear like the wind while the people continue to suffer enormous poverty and despair. The sweat and blood of the people becomes a tool for bargaining with foreign donors. The concept of having a government body that would seek to help the people is a concept lost to those in a leadership status within the Haitian government.

In order to understand the system in place in Haiti and the poverty that is forever destined with this system, it is necessary to take a closer look at the government. A close examination needs to be made of a system where the government is no longer in place to serve the people, instead has its own unofficial, self-serving interest. The people serve as an instrument to be used in any possible manner. Poverty of the lowest degree is cemented in the lives of the people of Haiti as a natural phenomenon. The distinction of being the poorest nation in the western hemisphere falls on the deaf ears of those who govern.

Those who are part of the ruling class have little connection with the poor and only serve to enrich themselves and gain as much as possible for their families' well-being. Those who are the ruling class, use every means at their disposal to maintain power and show little concern for the opinion of the foreign community. They are willing to allow their own people to suffer though the worst kinds of calamities. They have only one goal in mind and that is complete control and manipulation as long as humanly possible.

> Richard A. Haggerty stated, "In some ways, however, Haiti's political development lagged behind that of other nations. Its government functioned like a protostate compared with the more modern systems

that evolved in other states. Authoritarianism, typical among archaic states based on monarchy and despotism, characterized Haiti's political history. Haitian governments historically had lacked well-developed institutions, elaborate bureaucracies, and an ability to do more than maintain power and extract wealth from a large peasant base. Haiti's rural areas, where the majority of the population lives, traditionally has benefited least from government expenditures, and they have suffered for the past 500 years from virtually uninterrupted military domination."[29]

The possibility of change to this system lies in the influence of outside sources. The system in Haiti has benefited a select group who make up the one percent of the population. Naturally this group has very little incentive to allow change. Only a great heart, with an enlightened concept of seeing the needs of the people in Haiti above their own political interest of survival and dominance would lead to a change. Allowing themselves to be influenced by outside sources would be the first sign of a possible change of heart. Allowing outside influences on the elected process would allow new ideas to emerge.

Wyclef Jean said, "The future is dual citizenship, adding that many countries, including the neighboring Dominican Republic allows citizens to hold two passports."[30] Naturally, those who have left the country and have gained knowledge abroad could influence the process and make a major impact of positive influence.

The influence of the Diaspora would make a major difference in the country. The many Haitians who have left Haiti and been successful in other parts of the world could to help create a greater Haiti. Wyclef Jean champions this idea, allowing, those who make a significant financial contribution to have some influence upon the process. This logic forms the only basis to see true change in Haiti.

Wyclef Jean stated, "Haitians abroad should have the right to vote in their country, especially because they send billions in remittances to family members. If they are the ones who keep this country alive, they should have some kind of say on what kind of government structure there is."[31] Their financial contribution is one of the many reasons of the importance of given them a voice.

Allowing Haitians who have not been part of the ruling class to influence the country is a remedy to changing the failing system in Haiti. The system needs a form of check and balance from people who are not part of the one percent, who could inject some other viewpoint that would have a benefit in changing and making a difference in Haiti. Continuous outside involvement is the only way to prevent the continuous subjugation of the Haitian people.

> As Raymond Joseph, the uncle of Wyclef Jean, stated: "On Friday August 20, 2010, Haiti's Provisional Electoral Commission (CEP) rejected, without any justification or explanation, the candidacy of 15 potential presidential candidates. The list of those disqualified included former Haitian government officials including me, high-profile public figures like my nephew, Wyclef Jean, as well as doctors, lawyers, and prominent persons from the Diaspora.

> Raymond Joseph continued, "For some disqualified candidates, a constitutional justification could be argued, though the CEP has historically interpreted the constitution at will. In other cases, such as mine, the decision appears blatantly arbitrary, without legal grounding, and motivated by the political agendas of a small ruling elite."

> "My case is indicative. The explanation for my disqualification, which has since been provided to me after I initiated legal proceedings, is that I did not properly discharge my responsibilities when I resigned from office as Haiti's Ambassador to the United States on August 1, 2010. "[32]

There seems to be no shame in twisting laws and rules for the benefit of the ruling class. Raymond Joseph, a man who was allowed to perform his duties as ambassador, chose to resign to run for president, and immediately the conclusion was reached that he was not a good ambassador and therefore should not be allowed to run for office. The logic of such nonsense is unbelievable, yet this is how the ruling class chooses the next president. No one dares to question and claim that having a fair and free election is the right of the people and that the people deserved to be represented by new ideas and having the ability to elect the next president.

The political process in Haiti has to change to allow the Diaspora to contribute to the political process. The one percent who controlled the country in Haiti has to put aside their fear and understand that the sons and daughters of Haitians who have left the country, and have gotten a great education, can only benefit Haiti. Their knowledge and wealth should not be feared, but should be used to improve the little island. Allowing this source of knowledge and wealth to escape the Haitian people explains why the same group shows little concern for the suffering of the people.

What is the result of a system that is mired and controlled by one percent of the elite and allows very little participation from the Diaspora of Haiti? The system creates a process that is not fair and a government where the people are no longer at the center of interest. And very often the next president is chosen by the previous administration, and the will of the people is completely ignored or masqueraded.

Who will be the next president of Haiti? Will the people have as a possible first choice, that their favorite Haitian son, Wyclef Jean? Naturally, the people may not have their first choice since the man who is the most popular has been taken out of the race. The one individual who could have brought change by his very nature has been barred from entering the political process in Haiti, the one who would have injected transparency into Haiti's very core by the tremendous attention Haiti would have gotten.

Choosing the next president of Haiti is a political process resembling that of a theatrical performance. The concept of allowing the people to vote for show is noteworthy but, looking at the field of candidates, one can easily guess who the political power of Haiti will choose as the next president. By looking closely at the picture, and making an educated guess, one can determine who has been chosen by the elite to lead the country. **Jude Celestin's** chances are very optimistic, since in reality the one percent will make the final choice.

> The Associated Press article written by Chris Gillette and Evens Sanon titled, *Hip hop star Wyclef Jean disqualified from Haiti's presidential race* contributed to this report, "The commission approved 19 candidates and rejected 15, spokesman Richardson Dumel told journalists. While rejecting Jean, the board approved two leading contenders: former Prime Minister Jacques-Edouard Alexis and Yvon Neptune, who was the last prime minister under ousted President Jean-Bertrand Aristide and has been active in helping to coordinate reconstruction efforts.
>
> Also allowed to run is: Jude Celestin, head of the

government's primary construction firm and the candidate supported by President Rene Preval."[33]

There is no need to make a prediction of who will be the next president of Haiti, but it is very likely that the next president will not be the most popular among the people. Wyclef Jean, the most popular Haitian and the front runner has been taken out of the equation. The people's choice is permanently blocked but hopefully their voices will not be silent completely.

The most important criteria that could have made a difference have been removed from the process. Also removed is the idea of electing someone who is not influenced by the need to use Haiti as a source of livelihood for family and friends, someone who would understand that being elected is not a means to fulfill one's own ambition and enrich oneself as much as possible at the expense of the people.

Outside influence provides the means to make changes. The political process needs to be transparent and only allowing outside influence will influence this change. By no stretch of the imagination do the present leaders of this very troubled and fractured nation pay very much attention to any foreign influence. The leaders of Haiti turn a deaf ear when their own survival is challenged. Those in power have a greater will to survive than to hear the pain and suffering of the Haitian people. The tragedy and pain of the Haitian people become a tool to negotiate their own control and permanent survival.

CHAPTER 14
The Last of the Scavengers

GOVERNMENT CAN BE GOOD OR bad, but in Haiti government has been mostly bad since the foundation of the country. The Haitian people have seen the hands of government crutch the living the life from every sector of society. The future does not look good for a people who have known tragedy from the very existence of our beloved land as a nation. The result of eliminating our bright star, Wyclef Jean was no accident. Haiti needs a strong and reliable government that can turn the ship around 360 degrees. Yes, a strong government made of credible, smart, intelligent, and educated Haitians can make a long-term difference, with Jean out of the race one can only hope. These are the many important steps needed and the benefit a good government can provide in Haiti:

- A government that can re-establish diplomacy connections with other developed country is very much needed in order for Haiti to advance toward improving the lives of all Haitians, mostly those that are in immediate needs.

- Reform in the judiciary system is also a must, which needs to be reorganized and improved. The laws should not be sold out to the highest bidder. The laws should be made available to every Haitian, regardless of the individuals' level in the society. The laws must be served all of Haitians. Every Haitian, without any bias as their level of financial or education condition should benefit from a fair and well-balanced judiciary system.

- Justice is a fundamental right that must be made available to everyone. Justice must be top of the next president agenda. As an Association of 400,000 members, the American Bar Association unanimously adopts resolution calling for the human rights of earthquake victims to be upheld. The resolution was passed unanimously by the American Bar Association soon after the aftermath. The resolution is now official.

- The American Bar Association makes it very critical to the federal government to strengthen its effort to provide adequate food, water, shelter and security to displaced women and children in Haiti. Moreover, the protection of these vulnerable groups, in conformity with international human rights principles, is very critical.

Why is Haiti so poor? Before we start blaming anyone else, let's look into ourselves and how the government has function over the years. Let's analyze how Haitian leaders have been treating our Haitian brothers and sisters. Let's take a look into our government policies that continue destroying the country. Shouldn't we say it is our mentality that brought us down to such a disastrous path? In the past and possibility at this very moment, getting involved in the government was a quick way to make money or to fill up one's pockets, regardless of the on-going misery of the majority. As the saying goes, the government is a safe haven for individuals to change 6 into 0 or vice versa.

In Haiti, everyone is waiting for their turn to empty the government trust and run away. We have lost our sense of being patriotic. As we can see almost every president has to go live in exile with millions stolen away from the Haitian people ranging from Jean-Claude Duvalier (Baby Doc) to our infamous Priest Jean-Bertrand Aristide. The exile attitude is very destructive for the country. Why can't those leaders reinvest their money in Haiti? In fact, before they leave the country, their money is already kept in foreign banks.

The attitude toward investment is purely third world in Haiti. Of course, if those who have the money decide to put it in foreign banks, where would the local banks find money to loan out to small entrepreneurs? Those that have the money make up a small majority from the highly educated class who are, to some extent, foreigners that were migrated to Haiti and some long-term politicians. This highly unproductive behavioral pattern must be changed. The new government must establish some key indicators to assure investors that their investment will be protected.

The facts are we can do better as a people and a nation. The leaders in Haiti must realize that this disastrous selfish attitude must stop. It is high time that we changed directions. It is high time that we took a different path. It is high time that we started working together as a people. It is high time that we as a people learned to produce a government who cares about the well being of the nation. Yes, we must do better. It takes all of us to change the direction of our country.

A successful government must be very effective and trustworthy. We need someone who can walk the talk and talk the talk. We need someone with a solid vision for the advancement of the country. We need someone with a great reputation. There are a lot of great Haitians out there. We need a leader who is open-minder. We all know the job is tough for any leader that may lead Haiti in the months to come. Haiti's needs are enormous. We are highly capable. Let's put our resources together to pull Haiti out of this dark hole. We need to shed light on Haiti. Haiti needs a brighter day. In the words of Wyclef Jean:

> "I've said this before, and I'll say it again: The things we're trying to accomplish in Haiti might all come down to growth. We want more than anything to make sure that Haiti's children, its youngest generations, are given what they need to grow up strong and healthy and hopeful, and we're trying to make sure everyone of all ages has what they need to literally grow what the country needs.

> I have faith that this vision of growth can become a reality, but we know there's still so much to do. It's a good time to remind everyone what Haiti needs, six months since the earthquake, but, more than that, this is the time to commit ourselves to acting, before it's too late" Wyclef Jean advances.[34]

Endnotes

1. http://www.popeater.com/2010/08/21/wyclef-jean-disqualified-from-haitipresidency/?sem=1&ncid=sea rchusnews00000004&s_kwcid=TC|11111|haiti%20 elections||S||6200227713

2. http://articles.cnn.com/2010-01-13/entertainment/Yéle. wyclef.haiti.relief_1_haitian-born-wyclef-jean-haitian-people?_s=PM:SHOWBIZ

3. http://articles.cnn.com/2010-01-13/entertainment/Yéle. wyclef.haiti.relief_1_haitian-born-wyclef-jean-haitian-people?_s=PM:SHOWBIZ

4. http://articles.cnn.com/2010-01-13/entertainment/Yéle. wyclef.haiti.relief_1_haitian-born-wyclef-jean-haitian-people?_s=PM:SHOWBIZ

5. http://www.globalsecurity.org/military/world/haiti/ politics.htm

6. http://news.bbc.co.uk/2/hi/americas/country_ profiles/1202772.stm

7. http://americanelephant.wordpress.com/2010/09/06/ doing-the-same-thing-over-and-over-and-expecting-different-results/

8. http://today.msnbc.msn.com/id/38644803/ns/today-entertainment/

9. http://today.msnbc.msn.com/id/38644803/ns/today-entertainment/

10. http://www.prnewswire.com/news-releases/yele-haitis-wyclef-jean-urges-strong-call-to-action-as-six-month-anniversary-of-earthquake-approaches-98015304.html

11. http://www.webster-dictionary.org/definition/Refugee

12. http://online.wsj.com/article/NA_WSJ_PUB

13. http://www.bet.com/Specials/betawards09

14. http://thinkexist.com/quotation/we_can-t_solve_problems_by_using_the_same_kind_of/15633.html

15. http://en.wikipedia.org/wiki/Wyclef_Jean

16. http://www.voanews.com/english/news/americas/Wyclef-Jean-Challenges-Ruling-on-Haitian-Election-Application-101435824.html

17. http://www.csmonitor.com/World/Americas/2010/0818/Haiti-election-Struggle-over-Wyclef-Jean-s-eligibility-could-spark-crisis

18. http://numbview.blogspot.com/2010_04_01_archive.html

19. http://www.ajc.com/opinion/help-haiti-educate-kids-569199.html

20. http://www.sohh.com/2010/01/wycef_jean_breaks_down_during_haiti_conf.html

21. http://www.usatoday.com/news/opinion/forum/2010-07-08-jean12_st_N.htm

22. http://www.popeater.com/2010/08/21/wyclef-jean-disqualified-from-haiti-presidency/?sem=1&ncid=searchusnews00000004&s_kwcid=TC|11111|haiti%20elections||S||6200227713

23. http://thelouvertureproject.org/index.php?title=Jean-Jacques_Dessalines

24. http://en.wikipedia.org/wiki/History_of_Haiti

25. http://en.wikipedia.org/wiki/History_of_Haiti

26. http://countrystudies.us/haiti/64.htm

27. en.wikipedia.org/wiki/Haiti

28. http://countrystudies.us/haiti/69.htm

29. http://countrystudies.us/haiti/64.htm

30. http://open.salon.com/blog/thought_merchant/2010/08/15/

31. http://open.salon.com/blog/thought_merchant/2010/08/15/

32. http://www.csmonitor.com/Commentary/Opinion/2010/0909/Haiti-presidential-election-justice-on-the-line

33. http://www.foxnews.com/world/2010/08/20/wyclef-jean-world-wait-run-president-haiti/

34. http://www.ajc.com/opinion/help-haiti-educate-kids-569199.html

Jacques Guillaume was born and raised in Jacmel, the most beautiful city of Haiti. He is married to Mrs. Danielle Guillaume. They have two girls and one boy. Guillaume is the owner & founder of Solstice Realty. He is also an adjunct Computer Information Systems instructor with Jacksonville University (JU) and Devry University. He has a master's degree in computer resources and information management plus two undergraduate degrees in computer science and Management. He has more than nine years experience in project management, involving Continuous Improvement and Systematic Process Improvement and Problem Solving. Before leaving Haiti, he was an active member of the Rotary Club International. He is now the Chairman and President of the Haitian American Association for Advancement (HAAFA), an organization dedicated to serving, organizing and enhancing the life of the Haitian community living in the Northeast Florida region. Email: javdax@yahoo.com

Jean Jocelyn was born in Port-au-Prince, Haiti. He is a board member of the Haitian American Association for Advancement (HAAFA). Jocelyn writes from personal experiences about the problems in Haiti, and discusses at great length the issues concerning the suffering and the plight of the average Haitian. He has been active in programs and an organization geared to helping children, youth and the Haitian Community for much of his life. He has received numerous awards for volunteering work helping various non-profit organizations. As a Non-commission Officer in the US Air Force, he received the Humanitarian Service Medal for volunteer work in the aftermath of Hurricane Hugo. Email: jmjocelyn@comcast.net